Praise for *The Most Beautiful Disaster*

"Hope Carpenter holds nothing back in her new book. A life marked by trauma and shame becomes a picture of God's redeeming grace. This book is vulnerable and powerful."

—Pastor Steven and Holly Furtick, Elevation Church

"Riveting. Authentic. Deeply touching. This read is inspiring and touches the soul of the reader. The way Hope draws us into her life's story is impactful. Very few can do that effectively. She cuts through the fluff of our modern church culture to get down to the real truth—the maskless self that's exposed before God. If you want your life to be changed forever, READ THIS BOOK!"

—Heather and Cornelius Lindsey, authors

"Hope Carpenter, you've been reading our email! Okay, let's be honest. We've been caught fronting—putting on fake Instagram happy faces while trying to mask some unimaginable hurt from our past. Here, Hope reveals her own very personal trauma and shows us how to unravel our internal tangle of secrets and allow those old wounds to finally heal. It's time to get *real*: Nobody's perfect! And it's comforting just to know we're not the only one with scars."

—Pastor Nicole Crank, host of *The Nicole Crank Show*,
author, speaker, and cofounder of FaithChurch.com

"I love reading books that ignite a fire inside my soul. This book is a must-read full of broken dreams coming back to life, and it walks us through how God turns your scars into stars and makes your pain your pulpit. *The Most Beautiful Disaster* gives you a glimpse of what it looks like when God's mercy meets your mess. He truly changes everything!"

—Kimberly "Real Talk Kim" Jones, author and pastor

"This book is more than a compilation of pages filled with information—it's an instrument that introduces us to the God that redeems our life from destruction. This courageous, clear, and candid work will stir your faith and confirm the truth that God will bring beauty out of our ashes. Hope Carpenter is a gift to all who know her, and this necessary work is a gift to the world."

—Dr. Dharius Daniels, author
and lead pastor of Change Church

"Hope Carpenter's smile and contagious laugh would make you think that she has not seen or experienced some of the darkest moments that life throws our way. Even more compelling than her smile is her honesty in sharing those moments with us in her new book. Hope pulls back the curtain of her life, marriage, and ministry and gives us a personal look at what beauty from ashes really looks like."

—Sheryl Brady, author and pastor

"There are many books available that address the issue of 'Who am I?' but this book has a beautiful, realistic view of this question with a real-life testimony to back it up along with the Word of God! Hope is a personal mentee of mine, and I was privileged to toss my mantle on her. She has a heart for the Word, and I have great confidence in her. Do not wait to purchase this book and receive the wonderful testimony of a person who was set free and restored beautifully."

—Marilyn Hickey

"Hope's book is full of *hope. The Most Beautiful Disaster* will inspire you, encourage you, and change you! No matter what your circumstance may look like, this book will help you heal and move into your future stronger. With painful authenticity and transparency, Hope Carpenter shares not only her miracles but the heartbreak, the mistakes, and the misery caused from those mistakes. She shares all of this with the purpose of bringing you into the same freedom she has found."

—Dr. Dave Martin, author
and America's #1 Christian Success Coach

The Most Beautiful Disaster

The Most Beautiful Disaster

HOW GOD MAKES MIRACLES
OUT *of* OUR MISTAKES

HOPE
CARPENTER

New York • Nashville

FaithWords
Hachette Book Group
1290 Avenue of the Americas, New York, NY 10104
faithwords.com
twitter.com/faithwords

First Edition: May 2021

FaithWords is a division of Hachette Book Group, Inc. The FaithWords name and logo are trademarks of Hachette Book Group, Inc.

The publisher is not responsible for websites (or their content) that are not owned by the publisher.

The Hachette Speakers Bureau provides a wide range of authors for speaking events. To find out more, go to www.hachettespeakersbureau.com or call (866) 376-6591.

Library of Congress Cataloging-in-Publication Data

Names: Carpenter, Hope, author.
Title: The most beautiful disaster : how God makes miracles out of our mistakes / Hope Carpenter.
Description: First edition. | Nashville : FaithWords, 2021. | Includes bibliographical references.
Identifiers: LCCN 2020053581 | ISBN 9781546017486 (hardcover) | ISBN 9781546017479 (ebook)
Subjects: LCSH: Carpenter, Hope. | Adult child abuse victims--Religious life. | Psychic trauma in children--Religious aspects--Christianity. | Psychic trauma--Religious aspects--Christianity. | Forgiveness--Religious aspects--Christianity. | Christian women--United States--Biography.
Classification: LCC BV4596.A25 C37 2021 | DDC 280 [B]--dc23
LC record available at https://lccn.loc.gov/2020053581

ISBNs: 978-1-5460-1748-6 (hardcover), 978-1-5460-1747-9 (ebook)

Printed in Canada

MRQ-T

10 9 8 7 6 5 4 3 2 1

This book is dedicated to my husband who has *to be an angel in disguise. To have walked the rocky road of living with me during the years of self-doubt, confusion, extreme anxiety, living a double life, and all the while trying to lead our home, help raise our kids, lead a worldwide ministry, losing his father, should I go on? Ron, you really are the greatest man I know. You have always done the right thing, even when it hurt. I trust you with my life and I feel like I am the most blessed woman I know. I wouldn't trade my life with anybody. I'd rather be with you, broke and homeless, than to live with somebody else rich and famous. Our process hasn't been easy, not one day, but it has built us into a fortress that no one or nothing can penetrate. Thank you for allowing me to tell this story. My prayer is that our pain will be someone else's victory. I love you…*

Hope

Contents

Introduction

For my fiftieth birthday, my church threw me a masquerade birthday party. Everyone dressed their best—I'm talking ball gowns, sequins, you name it—and came up with such clever disguises to cover their eyes, from simple black bandit masks to superhero masks to elaborate jeweled confections. I wore a strapless red dress and a white sequined half-mask with feathers. My grandsons wore tiny tuxedos, and my friends and church family all danced and toasted and had so much fun together.

That night was the first time I had ever worn an actual face mask in public. Before 2020, when we all had to wear masks to protect ourselves and others from the spread of the coronavirus, it wasn't a thing people really did. But if I'm being honest, that birthday party wasn't the first time I hid part of myself. Truthfully, I'd been wearing a mask for many years. By the time we all started wearing masks, I was a total pro. Covering part of myself for my own protection was what I had been doing my whole life. I was really good at hiding what was really going on inside and showing the world what I thought it wanted to see. That was my normal. My go-to. Smile and look pretty, don't make waves, show the people what they want to see—I had it down.

I was a preacher's wife, after all. I wasn't allowed to have problems. I knew how to perform, and I knew how to make it look like everything in my life was perfect—the perfect marriage, the perfect kids, the perfect home, the perfect walk with the Lord. I had a mask for every aspect of my day. After a while, it became hard to even know what was real and what was for show. I got really good at hiding, which is why no one knew that behind the masks, I was falling apart.

I can't believe I'm here.

Why me?

This isn't how I expected things to turn out.

I don't know if I can do this anymore.

These kids!!!!!

I'm about to lose it all.

I'm the only one who feels this way.

I'm just not happy anymore.

What about me?

Even if you haven't said these exact things, you've most likely felt the feelings of despair, hopelessness, depression, anxiety, and fear that accompany these statements. I don't think there is anyone alive who hasn't been through some rough times and walked some rocky roads. There's no one who hasn't felt broken, beaten down, or afraid. If you've ever lived without peace and contentment, then you know what it feels like to be constantly longing and deeply dissatisfied with life and people and jobs and things and even your walk with the Lord. Nothing seems to fill the void, and you don't know why. Trust me, I've been there. I feel your pain.

This book is about how we need to get to a place of honesty—especially within the church—about how often what we see on the surface doesn't match what's going on inside, and about how we can fix it. It's about how we need to shatter the perfect images and face the jagged, broken pieces inside of us. It's about how spending our lives hiding behind our masks means we aren't able to become the person God created us to be. And it's about how to dig to the bottom of our brokenness and achieve real breakthrough in our lives.

Thankfully, by the time my fiftieth birthday party rolled around—the first time I had actually ever worn a *physical* mask—I wasn't hiding anymore, physically, emotionally, or spiritually.

THANK GOD. By this time, I had been shattered, broken, made new, healed, and set free. But the road to that place was long, rocky, and painful.

This is a book about how God can take your brokenness and your mistakes and make something beautiful out of them. I will share how God redeemed my heart, my marriage, my family, and my ministry, and how every aspect of my life is now flourishing in ways I never imagined possible before. And I will share stories of other women who have been in the trenches with me. I will give you practical tools that were shared with me and helped me.

This book is raw and honest. It might make you flinch, and it might make you think less of me. That's okay, because I'm no longer concerned with living for the accolades of others.

This book will challenge you. You're going to have to stop trying so hard to convince people that everything is great and take a good, hard look at the places deep inside you that maybe aren't actually all that great. You're going to make yourself vulnerable, and I know that can be scary. Been there, done that, got the T-shirt.

It's written from a place of healing, but not perfection. God has brought so much healing to me and to my family, but I'm not going to stand up here and pretend everything is perfect. I've got issues; you've got issues; all God's children have issues. We still struggle as a family. Our ministry struggles. None of us is perfect—but that's okay. I've learned that God is there even in the struggles.

This book is a testimony to God's grace and proof that He can take the most messed-up, broken, sinful person and not only heal them, but also equip them. It's a story of a real-life miracle.

This book was birthed out of pain, brokenness, and all of the dysfunctional places in my life. It is my heart and soul laid bare in the hope that it will inspire you, heal you, and point you toward Scripture and into the arms of the Savior.

This book will not hide the dark places. I spent too long hiding who I really was and what I was really feeling, and I'm not interested in doing that any longer. I have no tolerance for cubic zirconia Christianity—faith that sparkles and shines but is ultimately hollow.

This book is also not a secret path to an easy breakthrough. Real talk? I wanted God to wave a magic wand and heal me, but that's not how it works. God isn't a genie in a bottle. I had to put in years of painful, soul-wrenching work with counselors and mentors to reach the place of healing. This book is not a substitute for that real pastoral care or counseling. I learned so much from the counselors who helped me through my journey of healing, especially Lee and Denise Boggs at Living Waters Ministry and

Dr. Debbie Leonhardt, a licensed counselor in Taylorsville, North Carolina.

Ultimately, this is a book about how God took a total disaster and made something beautiful out of it. That's what He does. That's why He lived, died, and was resurrected so that you and I could live, die, and be resurrected too. So that we could trade our sorrows for joy. Our sickness for health. Our broken places can be made whole and our trials can be turned into our greatest triumphs. Are you ready to take off the mask? Shatter the glass house? Come out of hiding?

Let me hold your hand… You've got this.

CHAPTER 1

It's Time to Get Real

I leaned forward as the wipers slapped back and forth across the windshield. Between the pouring rain and the tears that streamed down my face, I could barely see, but I kept driving. I passed exits for Spartanburg, Gaffney. Any one was as good as another. I didn't know where I was headed, only that I couldn't go home.

My husband had just kicked me out. Ron said he couldn't live with me anymore because living with the news that I'd been unfaithful was just too painful. He thought that I'd lost my mind, that I might even be demon-possessed. And maybe I was those things; at the time I didn't really know. I was numb. I was in shock. I just kept driving down Highway 85.

Ron and I had started our church, Redemption, in Greenville,

South Carolina, more than twenty-two years before. We had started with a few families meeting in our living room, and the Lord had built it into a thriving international ministry. We had multiple campuses hosting over ten thousand weekly attendees, and Ron was preaching every week on television. We both spoke at national conferences and had hosted some of the biggest names in Christianity in our sanctuary. My women's ministry, Women of Hope, was growing, and I had invitations to preach coming in weekly. I had three beautiful children and a grandson I adored. I had heard God's call on my life when I was fifteen, and I knew Ron and I were following His path and serving Him diligently.

By this time, 2013, we had plenty of money, a beautiful home, dear friends. From the outside, it looked like I was living the dream.

And I knew, as I passed the exits for Blacksburg and Grover, that my life as I had known it was over.

I had just confessed to Ron that I'd been unfaithful. Not for the first time. He'd given me thirty minutes to get my things and get out of the house. My life and ministry were ruined. My husband was going to divorce me. My kids would probably never forgive me.

On the surface, it seemed like the worst possible thing that could have happened.

But the truth was, I finally felt free. I felt like the biggest weight had been lifted from my shoulders. There would be no more lies, no more secrets. I had finally told the truth, and it had—for maybe the first time in my life—truly set me free.

I didn't have to pretend anymore.

You see, I had spent my entire life presenting a happy, flawless face to the world while inside, I was broken. I don't think I'm alone in that either. I've spent most of my life in ministry, and I've talked with thousands of women, heard their stories and prayed with them through their pain. I've met female executives at large corporations who kill it in the boardroom but who inside are so insecure and scared they can't sleep at night. I've met women whose marriages seem rock solid, who inspire #couplegoals hashtags on social media, but who secretly resent their husbands or are trying to figure out how to leave. I've met women whose children show up at every youth group event and every prayer service, but who are secretly in treatment for addiction, cutting, or eating disorders. I've heard their pain and seen their tears, and I know I'm not the only one.

I never intended to blow up my marriage, destroy my family, or ruin my ministry. I never thought I could cheat on my husband or live a double life for almost a decade. But that's exactly what I did.

I also never intended to put on a façade. I never made the decision to hide what was really going on inside, and I certainly didn't set out to make everyone believe my life was rosy all the time. It's just that I had been destroyed inside for so long that the only way I knew how to cope was to make sure everything looked perfect on the outside. And after putting on the perfect front for so long, suddenly everyone knew what a total wreck I really was, and it felt strangely good.

The truth is, I didn't have a clue how to cope with the pressures of my "perfect" life, and I sure didn't have any idea how to ask for help. I didn't understand how the trauma in my past was still affecting me in ways I couldn't even begin to name. And I was not about to lift that veil and let anyone see how much I was really struggling.

Instead, I made a series of bad decisions that destroyed my marriage, my family, and my ministry. I messed up, big-time.

Maybe you've been there too. Maybe, like me, you're afraid to let people see what's really going on. Your transgressions may not be as dramatic as mine—it takes a special touch to do it as thoroughly as I did—but I bet you hide what's happening in your life sometimes too. Maybe you've snapped pictures of you and your little darling on a Mommy-daughter date but the truth is you spent the whole time snapping at her to stop wiping her nose on her sleeve. Perhaps you love to post videos of you and your friends glammed up and looking for all the world like you're having the time of your life when really you'd rather be home on your couch. Maybe you make a big show of how much you love your husband but then you go home and Google-stalk that cute single guy at work. You get dressed up for church, know all the songs, say all the right things, but God seems farther away than ever before.

Of course, we all choose how we present ourselves to the world. We all want to put our best foot forward, and there's nothing wrong with that. The problem begins when we can't tell the difference between what's for show and what's real, or between how we say we feel and how we really feel. The problem is when you start mistaking the images for reality.

The funny thing is, once my façade had been ripped away and I could no longer hide behind the picture I presented to everyone, I finally felt free.

TRUE AUTHENTICITY

Authenticity is one of those buzzwords that you hear a lot these days, especially if you spend much time in churches. Women's conferences are full of people sharing about being their authentic self. This is a good thing—the more we push to open up and really share with each other, the better.

However, going to a two-day "Live Your Best Life Conference" is not going to delete the forty years of experience that tells you being honest and vulnerable is risky. Real change, real deep soul change, is not a one-stop shop with a $99 registration fee attached to it.

And then there's this: Are we really getting to true, deep, healing authenticity and vulnerability when we share that we didn't get our laundry done or how long it's been since we've washed our hair or that we don't pray as much as we want to? How our morning quiet time was interrupted when we got up to make pancakes for our adorable child?

It's not that these things aren't true or real or hard. But I suspect that for most of us, our deepest, darkest secrets are quite a bit deeper and darker than arguing with our husbands about finances. How in the world can we ever open up about what's really going on when so much of what is applauded as "authentic" feels so...superficial?

This is not a book about authenticity, exactly, although that's part of it. I will encourage you to take off your mask and to get real with yourself and others. In this book, we'll explore how deep-seated, long-buried pain and lessons learned in childhood drive the ways we act today, and we'll talk about how we have to first face the brokenness and sin in our own lives *for ourselves* before we can truly get real with one another. Sometimes—often—the hardest person to be authentic with is yourself. We'll also explore the amazing healing power of showing our authentic selves to our Lord and Savior and asking for His help in overcoming the hurts and hurdles in our lives. True freedom involves being willing to take a long, honest look at our hearts and what is really hidden deep down inside there. What sin are you struggling with? What pain have you buried deep, deep down but is still driving your thoughts and your today?

REAL TALK ABOUT THE CHURCH

People in general do a lot of hiding, but I believe Christians are particularly good at this kind of pretending. We show up at church on Sunday and put on our best face and don't want anyone to know that we yelled at our kids and were rude to our husband just before we walked in that church door. We Instagram our devotions and hang Bible verses in our homes, but we feel disconnected from God. We go through the motions and know all the right answers, but it's been years since we've felt the hope of Christ or the joy of the Spirit in our lives.

Now, we all know that we don't glow in the dark, right? None of us are sin-free. We all wrestle with our own set of issues, and mine are different than yours and yours are different than your

None of us are sin-free.

neighbor's. If we know this, then why do we have such a hard time with telling the truth about what we are all dealing with? Just because we are saved doesn't mean we won't struggle. We don't lose our desires, just like that. I wish churches were better at giving people real help for how to deal with our flesh. Instead, more often we are made to feel shame and guilt when we admit our issues and our struggles and our mistakes. It's no wonder we feel the need to hide! That shame makes us afraid to admit our own problems, and the fear it inspires makes us turn our faces away from those who have fallen or who are struggling.

Given that we all struggle with the same forces and the same desires, and that being a Christian doesn't make us exempt, I believe church should be an atmosphere where we can be honest about our hurt and pain and get counsel when we are struggling. But instead, so many of us have gotten the message that we are alone in our struggles and we need to hide what's really going on to be accepted.

When I think about how the church makes people afraid to show their true struggles, I'm reminded of the man with the withered hand Jesus healed in Mark 3:1–5. Remember that story?

> Jesus went into the synagogue, and a man with a shriveled hand was there. Some of them were looking for a reason to accuse Jesus, so they watched him closely to see if he would heal him on the Sabbath. Jesus said to the man with the shriveled hand, "Stand up in front of everyone." Then Jesus asked them, "Which is lawful on the Sabbath: to do good or to do evil, to save life or to kill?" But they remained silent. He looked around at them in anger and, deeply distressed at their stubborn hearts, said to the man, "Stretch out your hand." He stretched it out, and his hand was completely restored.

This man had no doubt spent his life hiding his injury and the shame that came with it, and then Jesus came along and told him to stretch out his hand. I think most of us Christians would have stretched out the good hand, the one that *didn't* cause us embarrassment and pain. I know I would have! I wouldn't want anyone—*especially* Jesus—to see that I wasn't perfect. But this man showed Jesus the broken parts of himself, and Jesus honored that faith with healing.

We acknowledge our inability to hide from Him and the richness of His healing power when we trust Him with our deepest shame and broken parts. The true church of Jesus Christ creates an atmosphere where we can willingly show our weaknesses, our "withered hand," because that's the whole reason He died for us! Church is supposed to preach the good news of the gospel: Jesus paid the price for our sins because He knew that we weren't able to. A healthy church will foster an environment that encourages you to stretch out your withered hand, not make you feel ashamed or guilty when—not *if*—you struggle. So many people have fallen prey to sin because they didn't have a safe place to open up and be honest about what they were feeling and going through. God help us!

YOU WILL STRUGGLE, BUT YOU HAVE POWER TO OVERCOME IT

So many Christians think that just because they gave their hearts to the Lord, they will never have a sinful desire ever again, and that's just not true. Those desires do not go away. Just because we have been covered with the blood of Christ doesn't mean that we are instantly made perfect. Sanctification is not a one-and-done kind of thing. It takes daily—hourly!—doses of God's grace to keep us turning to God instead of giving in to our own desires.

I was brought up in a church where we were encouraged (to

put it mildly) to strive for holiness and devoutness. I spent so much of my life genuinely trying to be holy, and feeling shame, hurt, and worthlessness when I failed. I honestly believe that the pastors I grew up listening to really wanted to encourage us to live a holy life. But the problem is this: *Jesus is the only one without sin!* He is the only one who is truly holy. Scripture even tells us that "our righteous acts are like filthy rags" (Isaiah 64:6).

Wanting to please God is an important part of our faith and its practice. But all too often, in the midst of this pursuit of God's pleasure, we forget the earth-shattering, mind-blowing truth that God's love for us is already more perfect than the most sincere, lifelong pursuit of holiness. Genuine faith is not about trying to please a God who demands perfection; faith is about a relationship with a God who loves us just as we are. The deep transformative truth of living in relationship with God is that *God finds us out of His great love for us.* Where there is religion without relationship, there is striving, fear, and guilt, and the sense that we're never good enough. In a true relationship with God through Christ, there is rest and peace and assurance that God loves us perfectly as we are.

Does that mean we don't pursue holiness? Absolutely not! But we cannot be free to pursue holiness or to enjoy the beauty of our relationship with God when we live buried in shame, hiding our shortcomings and failures. I've been there and done that. Never again. I refuse.

On the flip side, when we start to think that "we're above that" or we're too holy for temptations to affect us, we're really teetering on the verge of destruction. Proverbs 28:26 says, "whoever trusts in his own mind is a fool, but he who walks in wisdom will be delivered" (ESV). There is a battle that we have to always be fighting, and that is the battle of our flesh. Our feelings want what they want, and our feelings aren't always truthful, nor are they righteous. My *feelings* want me to slap three people before lunchtime!

Here's the thing: It's no accident that we all struggle with our flesh and with the shame that our sins cause us. It's not just some fluke thing. We have an enemy. He wants to destroy us, and he will go to any length to lure us, trap us, and ultimately destroy us (John 10:10). I've been in full-time ministry since 1990, and I have had the opportunity to observe, again and again, that most of us Christians are incredibly naïve about our natures and the destructive forces in our flesh. Truly, we are "destroyed for lack of knowledge" (Hosea 4:6 ESV). Although God's Word commands us not to be led by our temporary feelings or to trust our own hearts (Jeremiah 17:9), we still fall into these traps.

But we don't have to. We have the power of Jesus Christ within us, and that is stronger than any scheme the devil dreams up. And God wants us to use it! First, we have to admit we are tempted, and cry out to the Lord to help us! We do not have the power to overcome the enemy's schemes by ourselves, but we do have the power of the Holy Spirit inside us and the Word of God to help us. When we pray, we are accessing the power of God to fight against the temptations of our flesh, and He gladly gives it to us. But you have to admit you need it and ask. Admitting that you need help, that you aren't perfect, is the first step to being changed, inside and out.

So many of us have spent so long hiding. Maybe it's time to start admitting that it's not working for us, that we're all hurting and broken inside but we don't know what to do about it. What would happen if we started being real with one another about the struggles we're all facing? I can't help but think it would be a step in the right direction.

I know from experience that when you don't confront your pain in a healthy way, it can eat you up inside. Even if you refuse to admit it's there, that doesn't mean it doesn't affect you. I learned that the hard way.

IT'S HARD, BUT IT'S WORTH IT

When I was in my own dark pit after my sins had been revealed, I realized that to get out of it, I would need to dig deeper than I ever had before. I was going to have to admit that I had messed up, and then I was going to have to rely on God's grace and fight my way out of the horrible mess I was in. I couldn't do what I'd always done before, which was dance around what I'd done, blame other people, or run away as fast as I possibly could. I knew that this time, I was at a crossroads. I had to decide to face the things I'd been hiding from all along. I was so sick of where the fake, scared, and timid me had left me. I couldn't live like this anymore. I was ready to do whatever it took, for as long as it took, to figure out who I was and fight for my rights as a daughter of the King of Kings and Lord of Lords.

"God, if You're really out there, if You are who You say You are, I need You right now like I've never needed You. I need You to help me," I prayed. Meanwhile, I was full of doubt. Could I even survive this mess? This devastation? This shame? This failure? Can God ever use me? Had I gone too far? "Please help me," I prayed. "I want to live and not die. I want to thrive and not just survive. Make me brave and strong and free."

As you'll see, it wasn't easy. It was the hardest thing I've ever done. And in the pages of this book, I'm going to show you what I've learned. I'm going to take you through the darkest days, when I was so lost and hurting and confused that I tried to find relief from the pain of my past in the worst possible ways. I'm going to take you back to the beginning, to the roots of the problem. It's not pretty, but it's real, and I've come to realize that that is far more important. We're going to dig into Scripture, because I believe that it truly is a lamp unto our feet and a light unto our path (Psalm 119:105). My prayer is that you will come to understand how beloved you are, exactly as you are. You don't have to put on a pretty front because there's no fooling the One who created you.

I have to warn you up front that it won't be easy. God delights in making beauty from brokenness, but don't think that you can just sit back and let Him take care of it. It's a process, and you'll have to dig deep and look hard at parts of your heart and your history that maybe you haven't wanted to spend time examining before. You'll have to stop trying so hard to convince people that everything is great and take

God delights in making beauty from brokenness.

a good, hard look at the places deep inside you that maybe aren't actually all that great. You'll have to make yourself vulnerable, and I know that can be scary. Believe me, I know that better than anyone.

It's not always going to be easy, and sometimes you might not like what you uncover. But even when it gets hard, I want you to stay with me, because I can promise you this: If you're willing to put in the work—if you're really willing to spend time digging deep and seeking God's wisdom throughout this process—you're going to find that your life can go from brokenness to breakthrough, and it can be better than you've ever imagined.

THINK ABOUT THIS

1. Just because you're a Christian doesn't mean that you don't have sin and issues that need addressing. We all have them, and no amount of hiding or pretending changes that.
2. Admitting you struggle is the first step in getting free. We spend so much time trying to pretend everything is fine, but you can't move toward freedom and healing until you admit there is a problem.
3. We are stronger than the struggle. No matter what it is that you don't want the world to see, God is bigger than all of it.

SCRIPTURE TO MEDITATE ON

The thief comes only to steal and kill and destroy; I have come that they may have life, and have it to the full. (John 10:10)

CHAPTER 2

Back to the Beginning

I married Ron Carpenter on June 23, 1990. I wore a beautiful mermaid-style wedding gown covered in sequins. It was my dream wedding. He was the best-looking man I'd ever seen, and what made him even more attractive was that he loved Jesus with all of his heart. He felt called to ministry, and so did I. We were going to go out and save the world. We'd fallen head over heels in love, and we'd planned our future together. We'd even *waited.* For three and a half years, we'd managed to keep our relationship pure. And as I stood in a glittering white dress at the front of the church, I was so ready to say goodbye to everything that had come before and start living the great life God was surely planning for us. I was sure my life was going to be perfect.

Well, it didn't quite turn out that way. Of course it didn't. And after years of counseling and decades of praying and seeking the Lord's wisdom, I realize now that a big part of the problem is that on my wedding day, I honestly thought I was leaving my childhood behind me. For so many years, that was all I wanted to do. I didn't want to talk about or think about my painful past, and I certainly didn't believe it had anything to do with the choices I was making as an adult.

But through the counseling I had after Ron and I separated, I began to realize that I couldn't avoid thinking about my childhood, because everything I was going through as an adult—every bad choice I made, all the lessons I learned about how a marriage should look, the way I thought I had to have everything be perfect on the outside, all of it—was rooted in the lessons I had learned when I was a child.

> The messages you received as a child and the trauma and pain of your early years have real, lasting effects.

Looking back now, after so many years of counseling, I can see this truth so clearly: The messages you received as a child and the trauma and pain of your early years have real, lasting effects. Even if you do your best to bury that pain, it is still there, and it still influences your life today. Your childhood home is so formative and so important, because the love you receive or do not receive in your home sets the stage for your understanding of God's love—it's your measuring stick of what love really is.

MY EARLY YEARS

I grew up in the small town where my parents had also grown up, Calhoun Falls, South Carolina. It's an itty-bitty town of about a thousand people right on the Georgia border. There were only sixty-four kids in my graduating class. It was so small there just was a flashing light at the main intersection in town. We didn't even have a real stoplight.

My parents were very attentive. We had a nice home, and we went to church every Sunday. I took piano lessons, dance lessons, voice lessons, modeling classes, etiquette lessons. They taught me to always believe I was meant for more than that little town. In so many ways, it was good.

On the other hand, my parents were very…let's go with *strict.* They truly wanted the best for me and my older brother, and so they had high expectations. I know they were genuinely trying to raise us to be our best, but there wasn't much grace if I didn't meet those expectations. If I did something wrong, if I didn't perform as well as they hoped, if I didn't make the grades my older brother made, there were consequences. I was never allowed to explain myself or offer my thoughts or opinion; I was just spanked or slapped or hit with a belt. I learned from a very early age that I had to perform to keep the peace and stay out of trouble.

We'd get a phone call from a friend's mom, asking if I could come over and play on Saturday. (Isn't it funny to think that's how it used to work? That doesn't even make sense anymore.) My parents would say, "We'll see." And if I got everything right, if I got all the chores done perfectly, if I didn't get a bad grade, if I didn't get in trouble, I was allowed go. At eight years old, I was tasked with using a toothbrush and Comet to scrub the tiles on the bathroom floor. And if one square inch wasn't to their standard, I didn't get to play with my friends. I didn't get to have the reward I had been working toward all week. My parents called it *being strict* and said that it was because they wanted us to *live right*. They were shaping our character. But everything had to be perfect, all the time. I later learned that my mother had been raised in a home where her dad traveled all the time for work and her mom wasn't very present, even though she was physically there. My mom didn't have a lot of oversight when she was young, so she thought she was giving me the training and discipline that she didn't get as a child.

But the message I heard was that love was conditional, and that set up a pattern of having to perform all the time. I didn't believe that it was okay to just be me. I didn't believe that it was possible to be loved only for who I was. I believed I was valuable, loved, and appreciated only if I did everything right. Of course, being perfect isn't possible for any of us, so I lived in a state of constant anxiety. I did everything I could to keep the peace, and usually that meant biting my tongue and doing whatever I was told. I would lie to avoid getting into trouble; it seemed better than the "discipline" that was to come. As a child, even though the temperature of anxiety in our home stayed on high, I knew that my parents meant well and only wanted us to succeed and live a godly life. I had no idea how those early lessons had affected me as a child until I entered into marriage and my new, "perfect" life.

My one comfort through all of this was that I always loved the Lord. I really did. I was saved when I was eight years old at a Baptist revival. I remember sitting there with my friends as they goofed off, but I was listening so intently. I remember that my heart was beating so fast and so loud that I thought everyone around me could hear it. I got up and walked down that aisle—this was a Baptist revival, after all, so of course there was an altar call—and truly, it was a life-changing transformation. A light bulb went off in my little eight-year-old head, and I just remember thinking, *Jesus. I love Jesus and I want to serve Him.* And I knew, even then, that I was set apart, chosen, for something bigger than me. God had chosen me to work for His service. I know it sounds kind of crazy, but I can't explain how God works; I just know that I've believed since that day that God had chosen me to serve Him.

And then, when I was fifteen, things changed. A boy I liked from out of town asked me out on a date, and I was so excited. As we were driving to the restaurant, he asked if I'd like to go meet his dad, and I said sure. We arrived at his dad's house. It was cold and dark, and he knocked on the door, but his dad didn't answer. He continued to knock for about five minutes, and still there was no response. I was starting to feel very nervous and said maybe we should just leave, but he insisted that I meet his dad. He picked the lock, and I was not at all prepared for what I would see. There was his dad, passed out on the floor, drunk, with liquor bottles scattered all around him.

I was scared to death, and I said I wanted to leave, but he

proceeded to force me down the hall to "see the house." It was only a four-room house, so there was nothing to really see. He told me to sit down on the bed and to be very quiet because it wouldn't be good for me if his dad woke up. Then he raped me. And everything in my life changed. Twenty minutes before, I had been bright-eyed and hopeful, excited about being on a date with a boy I liked. Then I was shaking all over and wondering if I would even make it out alive. I closed my eyes as tears streamed down my face, and I didn't open them again until it was over.

Afterward, he was just as carefree as when we approached the house. He smiled and said, "Let's get going on our date," as though nothing had happened. We got in the car, and I convinced him to take me home because I wasn't feeling well, and the whole ride back he sang and smiled as if he had done nothing wrong. I started to wonder if anything bad really had actually happened. Was this just what people did? Had I really been raped? I was so confused and ashamed and scared.

When I got home, I was afraid to tell my parents because I knew that they would punish me. I knew how they felt about sex. They were so strict. They would always tell me, "You're not wearing that; no, you're not old enough to kiss a boy; you're not going to end up like everyone else."

I kept wondering, had I worn something wrong? Was it

something I did? After all, bad things only happen when you're not perfect. Obviously, I had brought this on myself.

I had no ability to make any sense of the trauma, the pain, the violation, the fear, and the brokenness of being raped. So what did I do? I buried it deep down. I never mentioned it to anyone. That's when the downward spiral really started for me.

YOU ARE NOT CRAZY—TRAUMA HAS LASTING EFFECTS

I now know—after a great deal of counseling—that when trauma happens to people in their childhood and adolescence and they never get help, it leaves severe cracks in the foundation of their emotional life. It stunts their emotional growth.

In the mid-nineties, the Centers for Disease Control and Prevention, along with Kaiser Permanente, did a study of childhood trauma and discovered that young people who experienced trauma—such as enduring physical or sexual abuse, growing up with a parent who struggled with substance abuse or mental illness, or living through divorce or a parent's incarceration—have a much higher

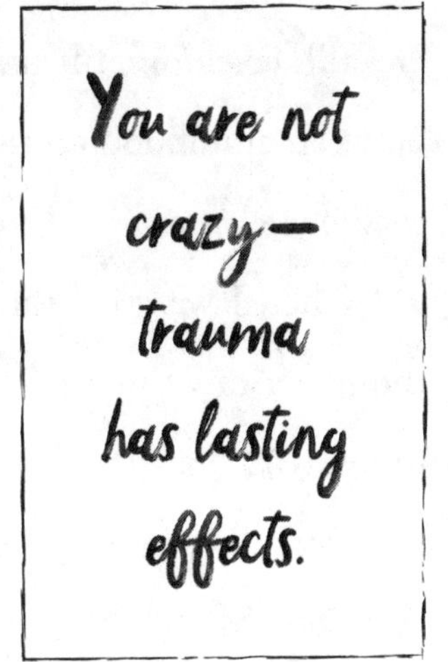

likelihood of poor decision-making, substance abuse, and poor health later in life. The more trauma a young person experiences, the more likely they are to participate in risky behaviors, like unprotected sex or drug use. Young people who have experienced trauma have a much higher incidence of alcoholism, depression, STDs, and serious obesity in adulthood. People who are exposed to a lot of trauma also have a much higher risk of having physical illnesses such as heart disease, cancer, and lung disease later in life. And trauma survivors also have a twenty-year difference in life expectancy.[1] Yikes!

I also learned that trauma doesn't just increase the odds of having poor behavioral and health outcomes; it also physically changes our bodies. Trauma can affect the immune system and hormonal systems and even change the way our DNA is read and transcribed, especially in young people whose brains and bodies are still developing. It turns out, there is a very strong correlation between childhood abuse or household dysfunction and risk factors for seven out of the ten leading causes of death in America.[2]

When I went off the rails in my thirties, I wasn't crazy, even though I sometimes felt as though I must be. I was dealing with unresolved emotional scars, and they shaped my life in ways I never could have imagined. Your own scars are probably affecting you, too, even if you don't realize it.

I didn't understand these realities when I was a teenager or early in my marriage. All I knew then was that I was so scared and ashamed and that I would do anything to escape that pain. I stuffed that awful first date so far down in my heart for fear of being rejected or punished or shamed. I made sure no one could ever find out.

My early experiences started a cycle that took years to break. When I was in a stressful, pressured situation, I would always cave in, lose my voice, choke up, and just go with the flow. During times of confrontation, my throat would close up, my eyes would dilate, and my body would go numb. The smallest of confrontations in our marriage would cause me to panic, choke up, and avoid negative consequences at all costs, even it if meant lying. I would adjust the grocery bill by a few dollars if that's what I thought my husband wanted to hear. Pain had taught me how to respond so that I would not feel fear. Anxiety had gripped me at such a young age; it was poured right into the foundation of my life. It steered every decision and every situation. Rather than stand

> Pain had taught me how to respond so that I would not feel fear.

up for what I knew to be right or even speak up about something I wanted or didn't want, I would close my eyes, swallow hard, and drift along until it was over, resenting the people around me. Being in this state of hardened denial of my feelings was still better than not being perfect, because I thought I had to be perfect to be loved.

During those difficult years in my thirties, I had a friend who was raised very similarly to me. She attended a very strict fundamentalist Baptist church and went to a Christian school. When she was little, she kissed a little boy at church and her parents shamed her to tears and dragged her to the pastor and made her tell him what she had done. She still told this story thirty years later with tears streaming down her cheeks and lips trembling. I identified so profoundly with her pain. We became very close friends as a result of our trauma and shame, and I understand today that we formed a codependent relationship because we had so much unresolved hurt and pain from our childhood. We allowed each other to "act out" and say and do things that we both knew in our hearts weren't right because the pain we both felt, and couldn't even really describe, was still haunting us. We were trying to give each other the unconditional love that neither of us had really experienced, but we didn't have a place of grounded strength for that love to flow from. In our desperate attempt to love and help each other, we caused more pain. We've heard it said that "hurt people hurt people," and it's so true. We are all broken people. Some of us are more jacked up than others, but we're all broken. And in our broken state, we tend to gravitate toward people just like us so that we can lick our wounds and find relief through this bond that leads to continuing the cycle of pain.

WE ARE ALL IMPACTED BY OUR PASTS

I've met people who swear they don't have trauma or deep pain in their lives. Lucky them—and I don't mean that sarcastically. They truly have defied the odds, and that's wonderful. That gives them a huge advantage in every aspect of life.

But even if you have never dealt with trauma or serious pain, that doesn't mean that your early years didn't shape you. Whether or not you have faced trauma, we all receive messages in childhood that impact us throughout our lives. If you grew up with a single mom who did her best to provide and be there for you, but you still didn't have a dad in your life, that leaves a gaping hole that longs to be filled. If you had hardworking parents who provided for you but they didn't love each other, you grew up learning to go through the motions with no tangible love flowing in your home. All of these experiences impact us as children and set the course for our future relationships in adulthood.

It wasn't until I got into counseling after Ron and I separated—after the years of going along to keep the peace and believing I had to be perfect to be loved—that I first heard of the ten emotional needs. These emotional needs are the ten ways a child learns to receive love,[3] and, as my friend Denise at Living Waters Ministries explained to me, how well these needs were met for us as children affects how we receive love as adults. It was so incredibly helpful for me to understand how the lessons I learned as a child about love were still shaping the ways I acted as an adult, so I want to share what I learned with you. I hope you'll find it enlightening. I know I did. It actually helped to change my life. The ten emotional needs are:

> How well these needs were met for us as children affects how we receive love as adults.

1. **Acceptance:** the need to be loved for who you are.
2. **Affirmation:** where someone tells you verbally that you are loved and have value.
3. **Affection:** closeness or physical touch.
4. **Appreciation:** having the things you do be met with gratitude.
5. **Encouragement:** knowing that someone is on your side and cheering for you.
6. **Respect:** knowing that you are valued as a person of worth.
7. **Security:** stability and protection.
8. **Support:** knowing that there is someone you can turn to, no matter what.
9. **Attention:** having someone be interested in you and what you do.
10. **Comfort:** having someone listen and sit with you when you're hurting.

Let's talk more about these, shall we? As you read more about these ten emotional needs below, think about whether your own emotional needs were met when you were growing up. If you find some needs that went unmet, ask God to show you how this might have hindered you from receiving love as an adult.

First up is **acceptance**. This means that when you experience failure or make mistakes, you know you are still accepted and still loved. If you didn't feel acceptance as a child, you may find yourself believing that your worth is based on how well you perform and try to earn love through accomplishments as an adult. Some people become workaholics for this reason, while others might have a poor self-image, believing they can never be good enough, or feeling as though there's something wrong with them. In my case, this eventually manifested in the development of unhealthy relationships in order to feel accepted. It might look different for you.

The second emotional need is **affirmation**. This is really about someone telling you that they believe in your worth. It could be your parents telling you they're proud of you, they're grateful to have you in their lives, or they appreciate something special about you. It could be being celebrated for accomplishments or praised for how hard you tried. If you didn't feel affirmed as a child, you might be performance oriented—still trying to earn that praise—or be fearful, confused, and timid. When I was a child, I wasn't praised for what I did right; my parents only found fault when things I did weren't up to their expectations, and that stuck with me. How do you still try to earn affirmation?

The next need is **affection**. Children need to be held lovingly and touched appropriately by both parents, and if you didn't feel this in childhood, you might find it hard to have close relationships or you might be perceived as aloof as an adult. Or you may go the other route and be clingy, needy, and overly flirtatious. The need for affection can drive some people to inappropriate behavior at a young age. For me, my dad would hug me and laugh and tickle me, and my mom would say, "Stop petting her. She can manipulate you with those eyes." I got the message loud and clear about how males wanted or expected me to respond to their attention.

Next is **appreciation**. If a parent recognizes when you get good grades or do your chores, they are appreciating the work you put into those tasks. A child who feels appreciated will feel secure in their parents' love. However, if a child hears only negative feedback, that child will often feel discouraged and give up easily, or be pessimistic or insecure. I learned at a young age that my hard work wasn't going to be appreciated anyway, so I got into the habit of not finishing tasks or giving up on goals. I've met other people who were never appreciated for their uniqueness, and now they don't even try for that promotion or ask for the raise. They believe that they have no value.

Children also need **encouragement**. They need to know that their parents are interested in them and believe in them. This gives a child motivation to move forward toward goals. If you didn't get a lot of encouragement, you might feel frustrated, withdrawn, or defeated, and you might lack confidence or feel like a failure. My parents did encourage me to be better than the average person and pushed me to take classes in piano, voice, and dance, but because of the spirit of perfectionism in our home, I never felt like I ever was really good at anything. It's a parent's job to point their children in the right direction, to pick them up when they're down. So many parents are just too busy with their own lives or still dealing with their own hurt and pain that encouraging a child seems like one more duty to do, and the child gets "lost."

Next up is **respect**. This can mean respecting a child's privacy or simply listening to them and letting them know that you hear and understand their words. Children who don't have this need met will often grow into adults who try to demand respect to cover feelings of insecurity, inferiority, or worthlessness. I often felt that my words weren't heard or believed and my thoughts and opinions didn't matter.

Children also need **security**. They need to feel loved, cared for, and whole, and they need a home where there is peace and stability. Otherwise, they will struggle with worry, fear, anxiety, and the need to be in control. When I was young, my parents used to fight constantly and threaten to split up. They would demand that I choose, then and there, which one of them I was going to live with. I grew up believing my home could be torn apart at any time. I didn't know if it might be the next weekend or the weekend after when it would happen, but I knew that I would have to pack my bag and choose.

Children also need to know that they have their parents' **support**, no matter what. They need to know that they're not alone and that there is someone they can turn to in difficult times. I grew up thinking I couldn't tell my parents when bad things happened—like when I was raped—because I knew I would not be heard or believed. I didn't feel like I could count on my parents to be in my corner during times of trouble. Rather, I felt like I was always being watched, judged, and evaluated. If you're raised in a perfectionist's home, how can you admit that you even need help or support or that you are struggling in any area? You walk through life isolated, alone, and fearful.

Then there's **attention**. Children need to have people in their lives show interest in and concern for them as individuals. They need their parents to spend quality time with them and with them alone. Children who don't get this need met may act out or get into trouble just to get attention. Some attention, even bad attention, is better than none at all, they think. As they grow, this may lead children to promiscuity, feelings of worthlessness, poor self-image, and obsession with appearance. I see young moms today on their phones, on Facebook, while their kids are running around, unattended. When their kids want or need their mom's attention, their calls of "Mommy, Mommy, MOMMY" are answered ever-so-kindly with "WHAT???" That screams "Go away." I mostly played by myself in my room, in the backyard, or in the garage at my nanny's house. A parent has to come into the child's world and not vice versa. A parent has to play games with the child, watch the movie that the kid chooses, get on the floor and play with Barbie dolls to give the child *real attention*.

The last emotional need is **comfort**. This means that when troubles arise, a parent needs to take the time to listen and give a hug instead of always teaching or correcting. There is a time for teaching and correcting, but it's not when the child is hurting. It means a parent empathizes with their child when they're defeated and sits with them when they're down. When the need for comfort isn't met in childhood, an adult may feel alone and isolated, have a hard time expressing emotions, or have compulsions or addictions. I was often punished when I messed up, and there was no desire to understand what was going on within me. When children lack comfort, they tend to turn to food, drugs, alcohol, sex, or something else to get the comfort that was lacking at home. I learned to stay safe by staying alone.

You may see yourself in some or all of these unmet emotional needs, or maybe you're one of the lucky ones who had all their emotional needs met. In either case, the lessons you learned growing up and the messages your family and childhood experiences taught you shaped and molded you. They shaped the view through which you experience life and how you respond to the challenges you've faced.

In my case, I learned that the best way to get by was to hold my true feelings in, bury them deep down inside, and try my best to be perfect and not mess up, or I knew I would face punishment. I learned that love was conditional and that there were consequences for not living up to an impossible standard. Those childhood lessons—though I didn't recognize them as such at the time—impacted how I responded to everything that happened once I left my childhood home and married Ron. Pain buried alive never dies, and it will manifest somewhere along the way.

> Pain buried alive never dies, and it will manifest somewhere along the way.

DEALING WITH YOUR PAST VERSUS CASTING BLAME

Now, I can already hear some people arguing here that I can't just blame everything bad I did in my life on my parents, a rape, abuse, and so on. And I agree with you 100 percent. I am responsible for the choices I made. I am not blaming my poor decisions and sinful actions on my parents or the things that I went through. I am responsible for how I behaved as an adult. You can't go around blaming everything bad in your life on your upbringing or the bad things that happened to you.

However...I do believe that when your emotional needs are not met in childhood, it leaves scars that carry into adulthood. When a need isn't met, a child finds a way to cope, and often it's not a healthy response. When a person doesn't receive unconditional love from a parent in childhood, they can't give pure, unconditional love away as an adult.

Now, after lots of counseling with my parents, who were so wonderful and gracious to admit fault and were willing to get healing themselves, they saw where *their parents* hadn't met their needs as children. You cannot give what you do not have. They were trying to pour into us from a very empty well.

Pain often becomes a cycle. We grow up in dysfunctional homes, sweep the pain under the rug, and then expect to run off into adulthood, relationships, marriage, and children, and somehow have everything be okay. But the pain doesn't go away. It's still in there, and it manifests in many ways as we grow into adulthood. This is why we have emotional breakdowns, burnout, multiple marriages, infidelity, addictions—the list goes on and on. We get trapped in childish ways of thinking and acting as a result of this buried pain. For example, as children, we may have pouted when we didn't get our way. We screamed when we were angry. We fished for compliments when we needed approval. If we don't learn to cope in more appropriate ways, we go on acting this way into adulthood. In 1 Corinthians 13:11, it says, "When I was a child, I talked like a child, I thought like a child, I reasoned like a child; now that I have become a man, I am done with childish ways and have put them aside" (AMPC). If these types of childish behaviors are present in adulthood, then that's a huge red

> When a person doesn't receive unconditional love from a parent in childhood, they can't give pure, unconditional love away as an adult.

flag that there are unmet needs and unresolved pain that has to be addressed so that we can walk in freedom, knowing that we're fully loved by the Father.

I'm happy to let you know that my relationship with my parents has never been better than it is today. We talked, we listened, we forgave, and we grew. They see me as a grown woman and respect who I am in God. I honor them as my life source and love every minute of our time together. We go on trips together, they stay in our home, we laugh, and everyone is really and truly living in peace. It's nothing short of a miracle, and it's a testament to God's grace.

I want to acknowledge that this outcome may not be possible for every family, because everyone involved has to want to put in the work to get it there. You can't control another person's responses, and they have to be ready to get there. But when all parties are willing, I truly believe that God can take the biggest disaster and make something beautiful out of it, just like he did with my relationship with my parents.

I also know that there may be people reading this who were abused physically, sexually, or emotionally, and restoring the relationship with their family may not be possible. Let me encourage you that you can find freedom and healing for yourself even if the relationship is not restored. As I will explain later in the book, you can forgive and move forward and become everything that God created you to be. God gives us this power, and He will also give you the grace. My prayer is that you, too, will be able to experience healing and redemption.

Ultimately, we have to accept the fact that we are hurt by people that we trust, by life situations, and by our own dumb mistakes, and we have to acknowledge that no one can change any of this except us. We are in charge of our healing, even if we weren't responsible for causing the damage.

EVALUATING YOUR PAST

How about you? Do you see yourself in any of the examples I listed above? Were your emotional needs met? Do you recognize any patterns of behavior that you can trace back to an unmet childhood need? I encourage you to go back through and rate how each need was met, on a scale of 1 to 5 (1 meaning the need was not met at all, and 5 meaning the need was fully met) in your own life. It can be very painful, but it's important to be honest and to look deep. It's also okay to acknowledge that your mom or your dad did the best they could, but there are still a few areas where you didn't quite get your needs met. This isn't about judging them; this is about understanding what's going on inside of you. It's about trying to get at the root of how you understand love and why you do what you do.

Acceptance	fully met 5 4 3 2 1 not met
Affirmation	fully met 5 4 3 2 1 not met
Affection	fully met 5 4 3 2 1 not met
Appreciation	fully met 5 4 3 2 1 not met
Encouragement	fully met 5 4 3 2 1 not met
Respect	fully met 5 4 3 2 1 not met
Security	fully met 5 4 3 2 1 not met
Support	fully met 5 4 3 2 1 not met
Attention	fully met 5 4 3 2 1 not met
Comfort	fully met 5 4 3 2 1 not met

For any area where you scored a 3 or below, I suggest you write a letter to that parent as a way of expressing how you feel. You could say, "When you cut me off whenever I was speaking, it made me feel that you didn't respect my thoughts and words," or "When you spanked me so severely, I didn't feel loved." **Do not**

mail this letter! This letter is not intended for the person who hurt you. It is intended as a way to uncover the wounds that are buried there so you can begin the process of healing. You may have to pray and ask the Lord to reveal instances that you might have blocked and can't remember. This will take time, and it may unearth pain that maybe you haven't thought about or felt in a very long time.

Once you've written the letter, I want you to release the pain. You can say something like, "Mom, I give up my right to hold this against you any longer. I forgive you for the hurt of not meeting my emotional need. You could not give me what you didn't have." I have included a prayer at the end of this chapter that you can use to lift your forgiveness up to the Lord.

Now look again at each need and see if you can identify the lies you believed as a result of that unmet need. Maybe you didn't feel supported, so you grew up believing you were all alone and no one cared. Maybe you didn't feel appreciated, so as an adult you believe that no one notices or cares how hard you work. Some of these lies may still be a part of the thinking that guides you on a daily basis, and any unmet need will affect the way you understand love and the way you act out and live in your adult relationships. I will address this more in the next chapter.

WHAT PERFECT LOVE LOOKS LIKE

Was that exercise hard for you? Was it painful to go back and think about the lessons you learned about love as a child? Maybe you were lucky. Maybe you were one of those people who had a great, loving, supportive family, and you're shrugging your shoulders right now, going, *What's the big deal?*

No matter what your childhood was like, the good news is that we don't have to rely just on our upbringing to know what love is. There's a wonderful example of what true, authentic love is right in the Bible, in 1 Corinthians 13. Maybe you've read it before. It shows up a lot in weddings, but it's not about romantic, butterflies-in-your-stomach kind of love. Here it is:

> Though I speak with the tongues of men and of angels, but have not love, I have become sounding brass or a clanging cymbal. And though I have the gift of prophecy, and understand all mysteries and all knowledge, and though I have all faith, so that I could remove mountains, but have not love, I am nothing. And though I bestow all my goods to feed the poor, and though I give my body to be burned, but have not love, it profits me nothing. Love suffers long and is kind; love does not envy; love does not parade itself, is not puffed up; does not behave rudely, does not seek its

> own, is not provoked, thinks no evil; does not rejoice in iniquity, but rejoices in the truth; bears all things, believes all things, hopes all things, endures all things. Love never fails. (1 Corinthians 13:1–8 NKJV)

This love is unconditional. It does not have to be earned. It cannot be taken away. It is not based on how well you perform or whether your grades or your hair is good enough. It has nothing to do with your sins and the times you didn't get it all right. This is God's kind of love. This is the love that hung Jesus on the cross for us while we were still wild, rebellious, and unruly, and didn't love Him back.

Jesus loved us so much that He blessed those who cursed Him and those who spat in His face. He prayed for the people who hated Him and ultimately crucified Him. This is how I describe this radical love: It's the love of the higher (Jesus) reaching down to the lower (me) and elevating the lower (me) above the higher (Jesus). Woowee…if that doesn't make you want to take a lap around the room, I don't know what will!

These verses show us what God's love looks like, and no matter where you started, you can rest assured knowing that the Creator of the Universe is capable of loving us perfectly. God's love never fails. God loved you when your past was still your future.

If you believe that—if you truly believe it, deep down in the marrow of your bones—then you already have the tools to understand how to receive love and give it. If you don't already believe it, I encourage you to meditate on this passage and ask God to help you internalize and understand, on a deep level, what it feels like to know that you are loved, unconditionally and without reservation. Warts, acne, cellulite, and all.

This passage also gives us a blueprint for what love should look like in our lives. Whether it's love between a husband and wife or parents and children, this love is patient, kind, and slow to anger, and it always thinks the best of others and always endures.

My hope is that, whatever your relationships look like right now, as you pray over this passage and let it shape you, it will begin to mold your understanding of what love looks like and will guide you as we go forward.

PRAYER

Dear Jesus,

I realize that many of my childhood emotional needs were not met. And now I realize the effect this had on me for many years. You told us to come to You as a little child, so today, I come to You as that little girl/boy who has a need for healing. Heal my deep hurt over the losses I have experienced in my life. I have been so angry at __(name)__. I choose to forgive _________ for ___________ and I choose to release them. They owe me nothing. Forgive me for wrong ways that I have tried to get my own needs met. Forgive me for sinful ways I have reacted when my needs were not met. I now realize my anger from unmet needs of the past has caused me to overreact today. I want to be healed and set free. I know now that I am not bound by the lies I have believed to be true. Today I come out of agreement with my pain, lies, sin, and unforgiveness. I ask You to renew my mind with truth as I receive Your truth and Your love. I know that Your truth will set me free.

Amen.

THINK ABOUT THIS

- Many of our adult problems stem from unresolved pain from childhood. No matter how far down you tried to stuff it, it may still be affecting you today.
- Hurt people hurt people. When we act out of our pain, it often causes more pain for those in our lives.
- Blaming others will keep you in bondage. You are not responsible for what happened to you, but you are responsible for how you deal with it today.
- Jesus loves you unconditionally, on your best day and on your worst day. Period.

SCRIPTURE TO MEDITATE ON

When you pass through the waters, I will be with you; and when you pass through the rivers, they will not sweep over you. When you walk through the fire, you will not be burned; the flames will not set you ablaze. (Isaiah 43:2)

CHAPTER 3

Who Do You Say I Am?

Most people will tell you that I have always been "the life of the party." I always had a smile on my face, and I was always cracking a joke and making people laugh. My parents say that I was always a happy baby and a fun-loving child. But how much of that "life of the party" persona was really me, and how much was a role that I had grown accustomed to playing? I've asked myself this question, and others just like it, hundreds of times over the last ten years, trying to figure out just who the person wearing that beautiful masquerade mask truly is.

In the last chapter, we talked about how the experiences of our childhoods impact us long after we're grown, whether we realize it or not. When I was in counseling after I went off the deep end, I realized how much I had internalized messages I'd heard as a child and how the unmet needs in my life led me to believe things about myself that simply weren't true. Let me say that another way: Because of my unmet needs and the messages I received when I was young, I believed lies about who I was and what I was worth.

All of us—every one of us—have heard and believed messages about our value, our appearance, and our gifts. We have internalized messages about our intelligence, or how lovable we are, or how important we are in society. We conform to roles God never designed for us and become people we were never intended to be to keep the peace, to gain acceptance, to achieve applause, or to "fit in." Sadly, it only leaves us even more broken and damaged, because then we are stuck on an endless treadmill of performing

> Because of my unmet needs and the messages I received when I was young, I believed lies about who I was and what I was worth.

and never being who God created us to be. These messages we hear affect how we act, what we say, who we hang out with, the careers we end up in, where we live, and so many other factors in our lives.

Keep in mind that this can happen *whether or not what we hear is true*. Maybe the entitled kid who grew up in a household with housekeepers and yard workers thought he *deserved* special treatment because of his last name, but he really wasn't smarter or better at all in reality. Maybe the kid who struggled to read wasn't stupid, he just needed glasses, but by the time he realized that, he'd already assumed the lies about his intelligence were true. The fact is, if you hear something over and over, you start to believe it, whether it's true or not!

The fact is, if you hear something over and over, you start to believe it, whether it's true or not!

There's even a fancy name for this phenomenon—it's called the *illusory truth effect*. Marketers understand this principle, which is why they tell you how great their products are over and over again. Eventually, they hope, you will believe it. Politicians know it, too, which is why they tell you the message they want you to believe, even when their words have no connection to reality or fly in the face of observable facts. It doesn't take too many repetitions for some people to take their falsehoods for the truth. Joseph Goebbels, the minister of propaganda for Nazi Germany, is reputed to have said, "If you tell a lie big enough and keep repeating it, people will eventually come to believe it."[4] When researchers have studied this phenomenon, they have found that even when subjects were presented with information that was clearly false—say, that Earth is a perfect cube or that an ant weighs more than an elephant—they became more likely to believe it was true the more times they heard the "fact" repeated.[5]

Most of the time, the lies we hear aren't as obvious as these examples. Our enemy is much too crafty for that. He tries to lead us astray by feeding us lies that sound enough like the truth that we don't see them for what they are. We believe the lie that we are not good enough. Not smart enough. We believe that we are dirty, or broken, or that no one cares about us. And when you hear these messages often enough, you begin to believe they are true. You internalize these lies, and the lies keep you from believing and understanding the truth about who God created you to be.

One thing to keep in mind: I keep talking about the messages you hear, but I want to be clear that I'm not just talking about things that are said out loud to you. Someone doesn't have to tell you you're worthless to make you feel worthless. Some of the most insidious lies are the ones that we intuit from the way we're treated, not from things that are said directly to our face.

My brother is five years older than I am, and the town that we grew up in was so small that everyone knew everything about everyone. My brother was very bookish and made excellent grades, all the time. I was also bright, but I had to work to achieve consistent As and Bs. School just didn't come as naturally to me as it did to my brother. I will never forget how some of my teachers made me *feel* by referring to my brother's ability. They put expectations on me that were not realistic because they were based on what *he* could do. I had different, distinct gifts that were my own, but they didn't want to see that. Even if a B was my best, I was made to feel inferior to my brother because he made an A.

When we allow the opinions of other people to define us, we live lives full of insecurity, self-doubt, and even self-loathing. Feelings are liars, and to come out of the darkness of those lies into the truth of who you really are in Christ will take a lot of work—believe me, I know—but you can do it! Trust me, it's worth it.

Feelings are liars.

HOW YOUR UNMET NEEDS MANIFEST AS LIES YOU BELIEVE

Let's look back at those childhood needs we discussed in the last chapter: acceptance, affirmation, affection, appreciation, encouragement, respect, security, support, attention, and comfort. You learn lessons by how your needs were or were not met. Let's say that your need for appreciation went unmet when you were young. If that's you, you might have spent your life saying, "I'll never be good enough." Or if you had an unmet need for attention, then you might have thought you needed to dress in a way to gain attention from the opposite sex to fill the void.

When I was a young girl, my parents fought a lot, like many young couples do. Hearing them argue made me feel unsafe, so to compensate for my unmet need for safety, I learned to be the cheerleader in the home. I would sing and dance and make jokes. I would do these things not because I was happy, but because I was trying to make *everyone else* happy so that they wouldn't argue. This set up a pattern where I started to think that I was responsible for other people's happiness. I know it sounds crazy, but really, how many of us go to extreme lengths trying to make other people happy? There's even a term for this (of course there is; there's a fancy term for all of these kinds of things!). This is called *performance orientation*. Performance orientation isn't about how hard someone works; it's about *why* they work so hard. People driven by performance orientation always need affirmation and compliments, because they are driven by an emotional need for praise or approval. If they do not get the praise or approval, they feel like failures, no matter how well they have done. Their security comes from what other people think of them.

I didn't know it at the time, but performance orientation motivated me throughout my life. I learned to please people to gain approval and security. And now that I have kids and grandkids, I can see how easy it is to accidentally teach your children these same lessons. It can even happen through common daily things: "You ate your vegetables. Mommy loves you so much." Well, of course Mommy and Daddy love you even if you don't eat your veggies, but to the child, obedience becomes tied to being loved. We don't mean to teach our children that love is tied to "doing right," but we do it. Our natural inclination is to say "I love you" when our children have done something right or accomplish something, so in their formative years they understand and feel loved when they've *performed* up to others' expectations. Their little hearts mesh together behaving well and being loved.

Your experiences are no doubt different than mine, and the way your unmet needs manifested as lies you believed is unique to you. But I bet if you take some time to think about it, you can see how the messages that play over and over in your head have their roots in what you believed about yourself as a child.

THE MESSAGES IN YOUR HEAD CHANGE YOUR BRAIN

We talked in the last chapter about how trauma affects your body, your health, even your very DNA. Did you know that it also affects your brain? It does, and I think it's very important to understand, biologically, how childhood stress and trauma affects our developing brains, because when we don't realize it, we can walk around with severe deficits that affect so many areas of our lives.

According to *Psychology Today*, there are three main areas of our brain that are affected by traumatic, stressful events:[6]

1. The prefrontal cortex, which is known as the *thinking center*. It is mostly responsible for rational thought, problem-solving, planning, empathy, and awareness of ourselves and others. This part of the brain allows us to think clearly, make good decisions, and be aware of ourselves and others.
2. The anterior cingulate cortex, known as the *emotional regulation center*. This area is responsible for regulating emotion and, ideally, works closely with

the thinking center. This part of the brain helps us manage difficult thoughts and emotions without being overwhelmed.

3. The amygdala, known as the *fear center*. The primary job of this part of the brain is to notice everything you see, hear, touch, smell, and taste and decide if it's a threat. If the amygdala decides what you're facing is a threat, it produces fear. When this area is activated, we feel afraid and reactive.

"In other words," *Psychology Today* tells us, "when we experience trauma:

1. The Thinking Center is underactivated,
2. The Emotion Regulation Center is underactivated,
3. The Fear Center is overactivated."[7]

When trauma persists, your brain ends up doing less thinking and less regulating of emotions, and being afraid more. Over time, stresses on these parts of the brain can lead to changes in the brain's very structure. These stresses then impact the way we think, respond, feel, and act. Your unmet emotional needs in childhood can have real, lasting, physical implications for your life. The way you understand the world is shaped, in part, by the way you process what happens to you and how that changes the structure of your brain.

In other words, your brain can be changed by what happens to you when you are young. It's trained to react a certain way to stresses and traumas, and you, in turn, are trained to believe things about yourself, whether or not they are true.

The good news is, just as our brains can be affected by trauma, with a lot of dedication and discipline, our brains can be rewired. (This is good news for you today. Get up right now and do a happy dance!) You can train your brain to overcome the deficits it developed in certain areas. When we understand what's really going on inside of us, we can have hope that things can get better. Your brain may have changed in response to your past events, but it can also change in response to the truth of God's Word and some real love and encouragement.

YOKING THE OX

Make no mistake—it is not an accident that we are so susceptible to believing the lies about who we are, especially when we are children. We have an enemy, Satan, and he wants to make sure that we never reach our God-given potential, so he lays traps for us early in life…rape, abuse, sickness, divorce, and so on. His desire is to stunt our growth and keep us yoked in cycles of defeat and brokenness. In *Easton's Bible Dictionary*, a yoke is defined as the following: "Fitted on the neck of oxen for the purpose of binding to them the traces by which they might draw the plough, etc. The ox is yoked EARLY in life intentionally to train this beast to obey and submit. This becomes a way of life for the animal and he is so trained to that yoke and the commands from his master that even though he could easily break free from the yoke and overtake the master later in life (adulthood), he doesn't have the mind to do it."

In other words, an ox is introduced to the yoke when it is young, so that by the time it's big enough to be able to break free, it doesn't think to try. It has become so used to the yoke that it never thinks to question whether it needs to be there at all. Isn't that just like how so many of us act? We get so used to the burdens of our past that we never stop to think whether we need to keep carrying them.

Many of us are still living under the heavy yoke of the falsehoods we believe about ourselves, trained by the lies that we accepted when we were younger, and we are still bound, unable to break free and really live. We don't know who we are or what we really believe because we're so accustomed to being who we're "supposed to be." Our belief system is tied to how we were raised and what our churches told us was right and wrong. You end up squashed into a box that doesn't fit and never feels right. You wander aimlessly through life, being whoever you need to be to make *other people* happy, while you seem to die a little each day. If your childhood was extremely traumatic, you probably are suffering from PTSD and are suffering emotionally more than you even know.

But we don't have to stay that way. Jesus said in John 10:10, "The thief comes only to steal and kill and destroy. I came that they may have life and have it abundantly" (ESV). If you aren't living the abundant life that Christ bled and died for you to live, then you are living a stolen, destroyed life that feels like a death sentence. I've been there. It's a hopeless feeling. An ache in your soul that nothing seems to fill. Louis Vuitton purses, Caribbean vacations, Prada shoes, or weekly binges at Target won't stop the ache; they actually make it worse because eventually a Louis Vuitton purse leads to five purses and Caribbean vacations lead to European vacations. Then it becomes vacations without your spouse and feeling like another person might make you feel better. You know how this story ends, right? Exactly. Nowhere good.

When you throw off that yoke and realize that you don't have to accept the lies you have believed any longer, you take that first step toward freedom. And when you do that, you can start to get to know the unique, specific person God created you to be. I've been there, done that—crumbled, shriveled up in a corner, thought my life was over. But here I am: healed and restored, thriving and living my best life. I never dreamed life could be like this. There is hope for you too. God created you to have abundant life, and He wants you to let go of the false messages you've been holding on to and to live it abundantly.

THE FIRST STEP

What now? Maybe you have never been affirmed or celebrated or encouraged and you feel like a hot mess. You have believed so many lies about who you are, but now, let me tell you who God says that you are. He tells us over and over again in Scripture who we are and what He calls us:

- You are chosen (1 Peter 1:2).
- You are beloved (Romans 1:7).
- You are complete in Him (Colossians 2:10).
- You are alive with Christ (Ephesians 2:5).
- You are far from oppression, and will not live in fear (Isaiah 54:14).
- You have the mind of Christ (1 Corinthians 2:16).
- Your needs are supplied (Philippians 4:19).
- You are God's workmanship, created in Christ to do good works (Ephesians 2:10).

- You are more than a conqueror through Christ who loves you (Romans 8:37).
- You are healed and whole in Jesus (Isaiah 53:5).
- You are greatly loved by God (John 3:16; Ephesians 2:4; Colossians 3:12).
- You are fearfully and wonderfully made (Psalm 139:14).
- You are crowned with glory and honor (Psalm 8:5; Genesis 1:26).
- You are the light of the world (Matthew 5:14).
- You are victorious (1 Corinthians 15:57).
- God has a good plan for your life (Jeremiah 29:11).
- God tells us that everything works together for your good (Romans 8:28).

The good...the bad...the ugly...the rape...the abuse...divorce...abortion...all of it works together for your good.

Do you believe these things? Do you believe what the God of the Universe says about you?

I hope you do. But I know how hard it can be to see the truth for what it is. I believe that the way to overcome the lies you've believed is to take every lie and replace it with the truth.

If you believed that you were not good enough, take that lie and throw it away. Replace it in your mind with this promise: You have been made perfect (Hebrews 12:23).

If you believed you are not lovable, throw that lie as far as you can and know that you are God's Beloved (Ephesians 2:4).

If you believed that your worth lies in what you can do for others, take that lie and stomp on it. God has chosen *you* (1 Peter 2:9).

> The way to overcome the lies you've believed is to take every lie and replace it with the truth.

If you believed that your life doesn't matter, know that that couldn't be further from the truth. God says your name is written in heaven (Hebrews 12:23).

If you believed that you are dirty or ruined, take that lie and light it on fire. Tell that voice in your head, "You are a liar." Scream it if you have to. Know that your body is the temple of the living God (2 Corinthians 6:16).

Take some time now and think back to those traumatic events in your life that might have caused you pain and damage. Then think for a moment about the messages you've internalized. What lies have you believed about your capacity to be loved, your talents, or your worth? Have these messages affected decisions you've made or how you've acted? How have these messages led to brokenness in your life? To really get to the root of these lies, you will have to take some time to just sit and consider the way you think. What messages are being played in your head? The term for that is *self-talk*. What is your self-talk? This will help you to identify any lies that you've taken to be the truth and what's driving you.

Jot down the lies that you believed, that still whisper in your ears. And then do the work to overcome them. Find the contradiction in God's Word and begin to meditate on those truths.

Pray over them and think about them until you believe them. Just as you can start to believe falsehoods if you hear them enough, you can begin to understand how beloved you are if you hear it enough. Go ahead, speak these truths out loud: "I am God's beloved. I am chosen. I am worthy. I am enough." Say these words until you believe them, because they are the truth.

As you repeat God's promises aloud, you'll start to reverse the physical, chemical, and emotional damage that has been done to your brain structure because of all these lies. Living under this yoke is not a life sentence. Just know and understand that it took years to cause the damage and it will take time to heal the damage. But you have to start somewhere.

If you've identified some of the messages you've believed about yourself as you've gone through this chapter, then you are on the right path in your own healing journey. It won't be quick and it won't be easy, but I can guarantee you, it *will* be worth it. Start today by saying no to your tendency to fall into the trap of believing that you have to have it all together to be loved and accepted. You are 100 percent worthy and you are 100 percent loved and accepted, just as you are.

THINK ABOUT THIS

1. Feelings can be deceiving. Just because your emotions tell you something is true doesn't mean it is. The devil wants you to pay attention to your feelings; Jesus wants you to pay attention to His truth.
2. Our unmet needs in childhood affect our adult relationships. If we don't do the work to unearth the pain we still carry and understand how that manifests as lies, we will never understand our worth.
3. We must replace the lies we believe about ourselves with the truths of God's Word about us.

SCRIPTURE TO MEDITATE ON

He who began a good work in you will carry it on to completion until the day of Christ Jesus. (Philippians 1:6)

CHAPTER 4

Don't Just Suck It Up, Buttercup

In the past few chapters, we looked at how our early experiences affect us, even if we don't realize it, and we looked at how we believe and internalize the messages we learn as children, even if they're not true.

In this chapter, we talk about how that brokenness and those internalized lies will impact your life if you don't deal with them. I'll tell you about the little early rebellions that started me down the path toward my disastrous infidelities, and about how easy it was to justify those decisions. Each of those little decisions made it easier to justify the things I later did and led me to live beneath my calling and far from the power of His grace. We'll also explore how your past is still affecting you, and how it can lead you to make decisions that you never thought you'd make if you don't deal with it. (I wanted to call this chapter "Now That I'm a Hot Mess, Watch Me Screw Up My Life," but my editor wouldn't let me. But I think that encapsulates the theme here pretty well.)

HERE'S WHAT HAPPENED TO ME

No one wakes up one day and says, "I think I'll ruin my marriage." No one says, "It seems like a good day to start beating my wife," or "I think I'll just go try some cocaine for kicks." Most people can't even tell you why they do what they do. In fact, most people don't even *want* to do the things that they do, but they can't seem to stop. Paul addresses this dilemma in Romans 7:14–20 (NKJV):

> For we know that the law is spiritual, but I am carnal, sold under sin. For what I am doing, I do not understand. For what I will to do, that I do not practice; but what I hate, that I do. If, then, I do what I will not to do, I agree with the law that it is good. But now, it is no longer I who do it, but sin that dwells in me. For I know that in me (that is, in my flesh) nothing good dwells; for to will is present with me, but how to perform what is good I do not find.

> For the good that I will to do, I do not do; but the evil I will not to do, that I practice. Now if I do what I will not to do, it is no longer I who do it, but sin that dwells in me.

When I acted out of my pain, I made some big mistakes. But here's the thing: Big mistakes don't usually start out that way. They usually start with small decisions, with little white lies and justifications for things that you know you probably shouldn't do. But over time, those small decisions can have big implications and lead you to end up far from where you wanted to be and far from the life God wants for you.

I like to think my own journey like this: I was walking down the path that I had chosen for my life. At some point, I made a slight turn to the left and veered off the path just a little bit. I had changed course but so slightly that I didn't even really notice. With each bad decision I made, I veered a little farther off the course I was supposed to be walking. None of the steps I took that changed my direction were very big in themselves. But over time, I kept walking and I ended up miles from where I wanted to be.

In the years before I took that first step off the path I wanted to walk, the pressure in our home and church life kept growing. The church continued to get bigger, seemingly every week. Ron kept getting requests to travel and preach. It was what we'd always wanted, and we were grateful. But when he was gone, the tensions increased at home. Our children were not easy kids to raise. We didn't sit in a circle at night and all sing kumbaya. Our kids were the kids that bit all of the visitors' kids in children's church and chased them around the playground with dog poop. Our kids were challenging, as I suppose all kids are in one way or another, and with Ron gone more and more, the job of disciplining and managing their increasingly busy lives fell to me. I showed up at every field trip and recital as I continued to play the role of the perfect pastor's wife—well coiffed and well behaved, always smiling, caring for everyone, radiating holy zeal for the Lord—at all five services, women's meetings, elder's trainings, and staff meetings.

And as for our marriage...well, all I knew about marriage was what I had been taught in our very strict conservative church: Do your duties as a submissive wife. I wanted to be a great wife and I thought that that meant submitting to my husband's desires and leading at all times. I felt that I went from my daddy's house to my Ron's house, and I went from obeying one man to obeying another. And there were unspoken rules in ministry life, too, unbeknownst to me. You don't wear shorts above your knees. You don't wear two-piece swimsuits. You don't wear *too much* lipstick (and certainly not red). You can't have *too much* fun. Rules, rules, rules.

Every day, I felt a little more lost. In my heart, I wanted to serve God. I thought if I could just be good enough, I could avoid dealing with the things that were making me feel like I couldn't breathe.

When I was a little girl, my grandma would cook beans in a pressure cooker. The lid was locked over the pot and the steam would build up inside. It would slowly boil and gather pressure until the pressure was too much for the inside of the pot, and it would suddenly let off the steam through the pressure valve. I felt like I was that pressure cooker, every day for years. Everything around me looked great! I was the sweet, happy wife who led worship, taught children's church, and typed the church bulletin (thank God we don't use bulletins anymore). I was the devoted stay-at-home mom of three who had the laundry done, dinner cooked, kitchen cleaned, and everyone bathed and tucked in every evening, right on time. But there was no peace inside of me and I didn't know why. I was full of anxiety, and I began to worry that I would always feel that way. Because everything looked great to the outside world and because I knew that I really did have a wonderful life, it made me even crazier that I felt such unrest and anxiety on the inside.

Then, one day I woke up and the pressure valve blew. There was nothing special about that day; it was just a typical day. But for whatever reason, I woke up and said, "I'm not doing this another day. I can't live like this or I'm going to go crazy." I really think that I had an emotional breakdown. Something snapped, and it was the beginning of my end...the beginning of the most beautiful disaster.

I went out and bought three secular CDs. People always laugh when I tell them that, but you have to understand, secular music was forbidden to me. I hadn't listened to secular music in almost twenty years. I don't even remember what they were except one—Jessica Simpson. I also bought a six-pack of beer and a bikini, both of which were forbidden in my world. And I went to our house on Lake Hartwell and I drank that beer and I lay in the sun, and I thought, *I'm going to have tan lines. I'm going to have a dark stomach.* It felt so good. Looking back now, I can see that I was just trying to grasp control any way I could, because I didn't get to make decisions in most areas of my life. But of course, I couldn't see that at the time. All I knew was that it felt like I could breathe for the first time.

It all started that day. You couldn't tell anything was different *at first.* But then I started making some new friends. I met some other girls at the church who felt the same way I did. It turns out, it isn't just pastors' wives who feel the need to put up a perfect front in church, who have to try so hard to show the world that everything is great while they're slowly dying inside. We had this bond, and then instead of being their leader, I became their friend. We would hang out together like teenage friends, except we were in our thirties. And then we said, well, why don't we go to the beach for a weekend? So, we would go on these girls' trips and let our hair down. This wasn't wrong on its own; the problem was we were escaping the problems in our lives instead of dealing with them. We would go places where we could act wild without anyone thinking we were doing something wrong. We wanted to be in a place where nobody judged us and we didn't have to perform for anybody. No one knew that I was a pastor, so I decided I didn't have to act like one.

These little rebellions—which felt like freedom at the time—let me escape, even for a little while, the pressure to perform and the fear that I wouldn't be loved if I messed up. They gave me the breathing room to live the rest of my life more or less the way I was "supposed" to. I'd straighten up when I came home, and straighten up at church and at the office, but I lived for the next trip, or the next concert or the next girls' night out, the next chance to do things I knew I shouldn't be doing. I didn't know it then, but it wasn't the girls or the trips that gave me relief, it was the ability to make decisions on my own, even if the decisions were the wrong ones.

And over time, the rebellions got bigger. Then there was a man. I started enjoying the time I spent with him—even though I knew I shouldn't—because again, it made me feel free from the traumas of my past and the pressures of living such a public life with so much brokenness on the inside. He was, in many ways, an escape from my real life. I didn't know how to deal with my pain in a healthy way, so I ran away from it and found a way to let myself forget, even for just a short while, the role I was supposed to be playing. I'm ashamed to say that our relationship went on for several years. I was living a double life, and that brought its own amount of torment and even more pressure. I knew I was doing wrong, but all I could think was, *What about me?*

The thing was, it wasn't hard to justify what I was doing. It was easy to tell myself that I was just having fun, that no one understood me, that I deserved to feel good for a change. I believed all kinds of lies from the enemy like this. I felt like I'd lived my life for everyone else, and now I was finally getting to do something for me.

Some people might call what I was going through a midlife crisis, but I now understand that this acting out was a response to the trauma and pain that had been sown in my life coming to maturity. I'd gone from my parents' house, with their strict rules and the need to perform to be accepted, to Ron's world, and that had its own set of rules and expectations. Growing up, I was never given the privilege of discovering what I liked, what I didn't, and who I wanted to love. I wasn't allowed to burn my fingers on the stove, so to speak. I was told what was right and wrong and who I could and could not date and what I could and could not wear. In adolescence, we are supposed to spread our wings and learn how to fly, even if that means we fly straight into a brick wall. We have to be given the freedom to grow and individuate and figure out what we believe is true and right. When this freedom isn't granted at the appropriate time, it will usually happen later in life, but it won't happen gracefully.

> We have to be given the freedom to grow and individuate and figure out what we believe is true and right.

Let's talk more about individuation for a moment. Individuation is when you have separated yourself from all formative influences and you become your own person. This usually happens to most people in their teens, and it is an incredibly tricky task. When you are a teenager, you are still a part of a family or household with rules, curfews, and expectations. Finding a balance between being free to become an individual and staying a part of the family can be extremely difficult.

While healthy individuation is not easy, it is necessary. Unless you individuate, you don't come to understand who you really are. Up until this time, everything we think, feel, believe has come to us from our parents or the people who raised us. Beliefs, habits, practices of faith, tastes, experiences—none of it has ever been ours to decide. Up until we participate in that process of individuation, we have simply emulated the belief systems of those around us.

Unless you individuate, you don't come to understand who you really are.

At the most profound level, this process actually starts the moment we are born; the umbilical cord is cut, forcing us to separate from our mothers. Going from a bottle to a sippy cup, moving from crib to toddler bed, staying at home and then going to preschool—we take little steps of individuation throughout our whole lives. It happens physically first, then mentally, then emotionally and morally and, ultimately, spiritually. This separation is a very natural, if sometimes painful, part of growing up, and the teenage years are the absolute crucible of this process.

However…for many of us who were raised in controlling families, the teen years is when the hammer really came down. The reins got tighter, not loosened, at the exact same period when most people are experiencing a little more freedom to explore. This robs us of the opportunity of discovery as well as the opportunity to gain confidence in our ability to navigate a complex world on our own. I can't help but think that if I had been able to individuate gracefully, at the proper time, maybe I wouldn't have felt the need to rebel later in my life, when the stakes were so much higher.

I have raised three children, and I know how hard this is to let go of the reins and let them explore, but we have to trust the Lord with our children and teenagers. We have to let them burn their fingers and figure out how close to the fire is too close. We have to let them make mistakes and explore their interests, passions, and boundaries. But we have to let them know that they can always come home when they need to. It's scary, I know. We love our children more than life itself and want to guide them along what we know is the right path. But when we parent out of fear, not trusting the Lord with the lives of our kids, we are stunting their growth and potentially harming their growth and individuation into becoming healthy adults.

Because I had never had the opportunity to experience the process of becoming independent and finding my own voice in a positive way, I looked for myself in transgressive activities as an adult. Instead of understanding who I was, I tried to define myself by what I wasn't. It was easier to grasp fleeting moments of freedom than to progress along the more authentic, healthy, and challenging path of doing the hard work of learning who I truly was.

During this time in my life, Ron began to notice that I had started dressing differently and acting different. I started keeping alcohol in the house and listening to different music. These things, while not wrong in themselves, were a clear sign to Ron that something had changed in me. He was confused and concerned, but I didn't care. I was grasping for freedom any way I could get it, and I was not about to let Ron tell me I couldn't.

He kept asking, "Where's my wife?"

I would respond, "What if this is who I really am?"

Honestly, I was asking myself that question. I had no clue who I was. I had always been whoever I needed to be to keep peace, to keep from being hurt and abused. I was who the church expected me to be: poised, perfect, on time, smiling, supportive, gentle, a good listener. No problems, and most certainly sinless. I didn't know how to explain what was happening to me. I didn't know how to explain that the wife Ron was missing wasn't really me. The first fifteen years of our marriage, I was just a mannequin—a shadow. I was miserable with myself…I loved my husband, I loved my children, I loved the Lord, but I had no clue who I really was. I had been performing the roles I'd been assigned. And I was exhausted, empty, and longing for experiences that would, hopefully, bring me back to life.

I spent these years trying to ease the pain of my past by living for me. I think of it like someone holding up a rubber band. For the first fifteen years of our marriage, I felt like I was being pulled back, back, back. I was just so tight and so tense, and the pressure kept building. And then, when I was finally let go, I overshot. Here is where I started individuating…but it didn't happen gracefully.

Ron and I were leading the church this whole time, but we were fighting a lot, and I kept thinking, well, maybe Ron's the problem. Maybe it's Ron's fault that I need to find someone who makes me feel good for a change. But things got worse and worse, and it got to the point where I knew they couldn't go on. Eventually, I told Ron the truth about the guy I was seeing. He had suspected, but he was still devastated. Totally broken. There were times the pain was so bad that I would find him in the backyard doubled over in tears. I wanted to tell our families and just get it out in the open, so we could all be on the same page, so we could have healing and closure. But he did not want to do that. He didn't want to tell anybody, because he didn't want people to know what I had done. I know he was trying to protect me. But also we had our church and our ministries to think about, and this kind of thing does not look good. We couldn't let people know what had been going on behind the façade. I wasn't sure it was right, but I went along with it, because what else could I do?

I thought that once I'd confessed, we'd be fine. But I never got deep, extended counseling, so I never got to the root of what was really going on. I didn't understand why I had been acting out. So, a few years later, I was back in the same place. Different people, same problems. Let me say right now, no one made me do anything, go anywhere, or drink the Kool-Aid. My own pain and brokenness were driving me. This time, though, I knew that I might not make it out alive. The devil's claws were firmly sunk into me and I knew that this relationship would not end well, and it didn't.

I told Ron everything. That's when he kicked me out. He was still grieving from the first time, and here I come with this news.

He thought I'd literally lost my mind. He didn't know how I could do this—*again*—to him, to our kids, to the church. And honestly, I didn't know either. I literally could not understand what was going on with me. Ron couldn't bear the pain of living with me and he had no idea what I would do next. He had to draw a line for his own sanity and for the sake of our family and ministry.

I'M MESSED UP; YOU'RE MESSED UP

From where I sit now, knowing what I know about how our past trauma drives our future actions, none of this is surprising. It doesn't always play out like it did for me, but it will affect you.

Through the years I've spoken with many couples who are struggling. I think of one couple in particular who were going through the exact same issues Ron and I had early in our marriage. I see it so plainly...she was raised in a very conservative home where she wasn't allowed to wear pants or makeup. Her father literally told her as a child that he wished that she was a boy. She spent all of her life trying to make her dad love her and accept her for the beautiful young woman that she was, to no avail. She married the boyfriend of her youth, the only man she'd ever kissed. They had several kids, and on the surface, she seemed to be the perfect wife. Then one day, an older man (read: father figure) started showing her attention and affirmed her, and now she's divorcing her husband who loves her dearly. I'm still trying to help her see the lure, the trap, but guess what? She has to figure this out on her own…burn her own fingers. I just don't know if her husband can take the pain of waiting. I'm writing this book for people like her. If my pain can help you understand your pain and help you to see and process what is leading you to feel the way you feel, then it's worth all that I had to go through.

In my case, I couldn't take the internal anxiety and turmoil another day, and I acted out to try to make myself feel better—let off the steam, so to speak. For some people who get frustrated by the direction of their lives, it looks different. I know some people who started to doubt the direction God wanted for them and decided to take matters into their own hands.

I have a friend who has such a gentle, nurturing spirit. She loves children and always volunteered in the nursery, and people were always telling her she would make such a good mother. But the years went by and she hadn't found a godly man, and as she neared her midthirties, she panicked and ended up marrying a man who didn't treat her well. The signs were there all along, but she overlooked them because she wanted to be a mother so badly. The good news? Her friends were right. She is an amazing mother to two adorable little boys, and she is raising them in the Word.

The bad news is, things got really ugly before she had the courage to leave her husband. She told me that she wonders what might have happened if she had waited and trusted God's timing instead of rushing to marry a man who was incapable of loving her as she needed to be loved.

You can see examples of this tendency toward rebellion in Scripture as well. Remember Sarah, wife of Abraham? God had promised Abraham that his descendants would be as numerous as the stars in the sky. But as the years went along and there was no baby, Sarah's pain built up. She wanted that child so desperately, and when it didn't happen, Sarah started to doubt God's promises and began to act out of her pain. She grew impatient, and she told Abraham to go off and sleep with her servant Hagar, and Sarah would just take her baby. Sure, seems reasonable enough. So Hagar gave birth to Ishmael, and they became one big happy family.

No, wait. That's actually not what happened. Once Hagar got pregnant, Sarah got jealous and started going on about how Hagar kept looking at her funny, and Hagar ended up running off into the desert. Only an angel visited Hagar in the desert and ordered her back, telling her she would have a wild son and to call him Ishmael. So Hagar went back.

Well, I can imagine there was some tension in that household after that, but we don't get the details. All we know is that

Ishmael was fine and all, but he was not what God had in mind for Abraham's legacy. Fast-forward to Abraham at age ninety-nine. Abraham had long given up on God's promise. But then God appeared to Abraham (probably scaring his Depends right off of him) and confirmed His prophecy to Abraham, saying that Sarah, now aged ninety, would bear a son. Both Sarah and Abraham thought this was hilarious, but lo and behold, nine months later, Sarah held newborn Isaac in her arms. This, then, was the child that God had promised them all those years ago. This was the child God would use to build the nation of Israel. If Sarah had only waited and trusted instead of taking matters into her own hands, they all would have been saved from a lot of heartache. If Sarah had believed what God had told her she was—the Mother of Nations—instead of what the circumstances of her life dictated she was, everything would have been different.

Let's be clear about this: Sarah never ceased to be everything God said she was, even when she was trying to take her servant's baby as her own. God's love for her wasn't any less true simply because she couldn't see it. It's the same for you. You are no less beloved, no less cherished, when you are acting out of your pain. Everything God says you are is still true, no matter how badly you mess up. No matter how far you might be right now from the path you wanted to walk. No matter how much you sin.

Sin means "to miss the mark." All of us have sinned and fallen short of the glory (reflection) of God (Romans 3:23). We can't just pretend sin doesn't happen, and we are especially likely to sin—to do something that separates us from God—when we are acting from a place of pain.

The thing is, sin grieves God, but not for the reasons people often assume. I know some people look at God as some threatening rule enforcer in the sky, waiting to lash out and strike you with thunderbolts when you mess up. But I don't believe that's what God is like at all. I honestly believe that God is pained when we turn from our path because we inevitably end up not living up to the uniquely designed individual God made us to be. The good news is, "All things work together for good to them that love God, to them who are the called according to *his* purpose" (emphasis King James') (Romans 8:28 KJV). Even when you make mistakes, God uses those for good in the end. I'm living proof of that.

> You are no less beloved, no less cherished, when you are acting out of your pain.

WARNING SIGNS

Like I've said, people don't usually just wake up one day and decide to ruin their lives. It happens slowly, and there are some red flags that you might notice along the way. I'm going to share them with you now, and if you find yourself saying or thinking any of these things, I encourage you to seek counseling before you get very far off track.

The first is if you find yourself *consumed with yourself,* saying, "What about me?" or "I deserve to be happy" or "I'm tired of living for everybody else." If you're saying those things, that's you crying out for help. You're crying out to individuate, but it's out of season, and if you pursue that...you're gonna crash and burn. If that's you, I hope you'll step back and take a look at your life and think about why you feel this way. Are there patterns in your life you need to break? Do you have unresolved pain from childhood? Do you need some time to figure out who you really are, apart from the roles you've been assigned? Do you feel like you have to perform for others all the time? If this describes your life, please, get help. Reach out to a Christian counselor or therapist who can help you get to the root of what's really going on underneath those statements. At the end of this book is a list of resources that helped me.

I am an advocate for getting mental and emotional help.

We are told to get a yearly physical to make sure everything is working properly in our body and to make sure there are no diseases that have gone undetected, but what about our emotional health? Or our mental health? I just want to break that negative stigma right now. God made us a three-part being—body, soul, and spirit—and we need to do everything we can to make sure all three parts of us are working properly. Get to the doctor! Get to counseling, and get in the Word!

The next red flag is *your tone*. How do you respond to people? I'm talking about being quickly offended for reasons that may not even be obvious. For instance, maybe your husband says, "What do you mean we're going out to eat again tonight?" There could be all kinds of reasons you're planning on going out instead of cooking. Maybe you haven't had time to go to the grocery store. Maybe you did go but forgot to get a key ingredient. Maybe you wanted to cook, but you spent the afternoon helping your daughter with an unexpected school project and didn't get things started on time. Maybe a crisis came up with a friend, or soccer practice ran late, or you started to cook and burned the noodles. But if, when your husband asks why you're going out again, instead of explaining, your first response is, "Do I not have a right to have a night off? You just want me to cook all the time, just like your MOTHER did?" *Hmmmm*...you might need to pay attention to that. What's really behind those words and that tone of voice? Maybe you were the little girl who had to have dinner on the table every single night, and when your husband asks the question, you hear Daddy. That tone you used may indicate that you've got issues in your heart you need to look at.

Secrets are also red flags. Anytime you think it's okay to have secrets, even if it's something small, like, *Well, I don't have to tell him how much I spent at Target*, that's a red flag. The blinking red light on the dashboard of your life that is warning you that something is wrong. In a healthy relationship, if you're really okay, you don't need to keep secrets from each other. If you're keeping secrets, that's just going underground, and truth is essential for freedom. You can't live in hiding, you can't live in a hat and mask, and you can't live in lies. Satan traffics in darkness, hidden places, and so do lies. Truth is the only thing that makes us free (John 8:32).

> Truth is the only thing that makes us free.

If you recognize any of these red flags in your own life, you may have turned just a few degrees from the path you want to be walking. Or maybe you're about to. You may be in a pressure-cooker situation like the one I described. If you see yourself in any of this, please get help, before you blow up and destroy everything and everyone around you.

I know—believe me, I know—that there is a stigma within the church around counseling. We put so much pressure on people to have it all together, and it's not healthy or even logical. We don't make it easy for people to say they need help. We make people feel like if they have Jesus, that should be enough, and if you have problems He can't solve, you must not be in a right relationship with Him. It must be your fault. You *obviously* must have a "sin" problem. But that's not true at all. If you have Jesus in your life, you're forgiven, and the Holy Spirit will lead you and guide you, guide you to other people who can help you see what you can't seem to see for yourself. The Bible says there's wisdom in a multitude of counselors (Proverbs 11:14). It's healthy to talk to someone who can help you understand what's really going on behind your behavior. If you are lost and confused, how do think you can make the right decisions on your own?

I know, it's scary to raise your hand and say, "I need help." I didn't even realize I needed help, but I can't help but wonder what might have been different if I had recognized the red flags and known to talk with a therapist or a counselor before I made the first bad decision. It might have changed everything. If the idea of calling in a therapist is too much, maybe start by telling a trusted friend how you really feel. Just opening up and putting your struggle into words can be powerful and get the truth out there. Maybe you can talk to your pastor or someone else you trust at your church. I hope you'll eventually work up the courage to talk to someone who has been trained to help you uncover those underlying issues, but any time you open up and get the truth out there, it's a step in the right direction.

One last red flag. *Friends.* Are you telling your problems to those who can fix them, or to those who only fan the flame? Proverbs tells us, "He that walketh with wise men shall be wise: but a companion of fools shall be destroyed" (Proverbs 13:20 KJV). Have you ever heard the sayings *Birds of a feather flock together*, or *If you lie down with dogs, you get up with fleas*, or *He who has your ear has your future*? We need to examine who we are hanging with and who we gravitate toward, and why. Are they friends who lift you up? Or do you spend time with these people because they let you get away with things others wouldn't? Sometimes you will have to make the hard decision to break ties so that you can start over and begin your healing journey. When true healing and freedom come, you will not tolerate living with people who hold you back any longer, nor will you want to spend time with the people who live beneath their calling either.

A true friend will hold you accountable. If you're starting to veer off your path, a real friend will call you on it and ask what's really going on. She will listen without judgment, pore over Scripture with you to look for godly wisdom, and pray with you. She will warn you when you're doing something that makes you act against your vows or your morals. She will speak the truth in love, even if you don't want to hear it. That's the key thing here—*in love*. When you're in the moment, it sure doesn't seem like love to have someone tell you you're being an idiot. It seems like she's a big meanie who just doesn't get you and hasn't matured like you have and can't see that the world has changed and maybe she is just too spiritually minded to be any earthly good, right?

> A true friend will hold you accountable.

But the truth is, it's hard to call someone out on their personal life, and only someone who truly loves you will take that risk. If someone does work up the courage to tell you they've noticed a change in your behavior and are concerned about it, please try to listen. That's a true friend. That's someone who loves you enough to risk upsetting you. And if you have friends who aren't encouraging you to behave in a way that brings honor to you, your family, and God, or if you have friends who might even be encouraging you to do things that compromise your values, those aren't true friends. Get yourself out of that situation as quickly as possible, because they do not have your best interest at heart.

THERE IS HOPE AHEAD

I hope this chapter didn't leave you feeling beaten down and disheartened. I pray it did the opposite. I hope it will shine some light into the places where you have been walking in darkness and help you to see and really understand what happens when you feel yourself act out of your pain. Because the thing is, I made some huge mistakes—I broke my husband's heart, I shattered our family, I ruined the opportunity to be a source of wisdom and encouragement to the people who looked up to me and counted on me. But God didn't leave me there. God wasn't finished with me yet, and He's not finished with you either.

God loves you, sin, brokenness, pain, and all. Period. And small or big, God can redeem our mistakes. It doesn't matter if you've just barely stepped off your path or whether you're miles from where you thought you were headed. God can heal us and set us on the right path. After all, that's why Jesus had to come. God knew we were going to need Him so badly. God *knew* we were going to screw things up royally. He knew we were going to act out of our pain and hurt one another. He knew we would break our marriage vows and traumatize our families. He knew it all, and because He loves us more than we can ever imagine, He did the one thing that would cause Him the most pain and sent His son to redeem all of it.

> God loves you, sin, brokenness, pain, and all. Period.

And He does. I know firsthand that He can take the most terrible, messed-up, heartbreaking disaster and make a miracle out of it. I know because He did it for me. Just wait until you see what He did next.

THINK ABOUT THIS

- If we don't deal with our brokenness, it will affect us and everyone around us.
- The steps that take you far off the path you wanted to walk often start very small. You may not even notice that you've turned away from where you wanted to go.
- We must individuate in the proper season of life or we will do it looking like a hot mess later in life.
- There are some red flags to pay attention to: Asking "What about me?" Also, pay attention to your tone when asked about what you're doing. Keeping secrets leads to no good, and your friends should be looking out for you, not encouraging you to move away from where you want to be. Surround yourself with people who can pray you out of a bad situation rather than get you into one.

SCRIPTURE TO MEDITATE ON

Whoever finds their life will lose it, and whoever loses their life for my sake will find it. (Matthew 10:39)

CHAPTER 5

Knock, Knock

God loves you, sin, brokenness, mess-ups, and all. If you take nothing else from this book, please nestle that truth in your heart and believe it.

But that doesn't mean life will be perfect. Eventually, our mistakes will catch up with us, and there will be times when we will fall flat on our faces. It's going to hurt. That's what happened when I confessed my infidelities to Ron and he kicked me out. The days that followed were the lowest time of my life. Some people call this hitting rock bottom. I call it living in my own deep dark pit. However, no matter what you call it, we are not left alone in these dark moments. In fact, I think these moments of despair and hurt and pain are some of the most important in our entire journey. These moments are God's way of getting our attention.

And that's not because God is some big bully who sends hard things to get us to pay attention to him. God is not some abusive parent who jerks you by the hair to get you to look up from your iPhone. It's more that when things are going well in our lives, we don't tend to pay as much attention to Him. We don't pray and seek His wisdom and spend time in the Word, trying to discern whether we're walking on the path God wants us to. It's usually when things don't go well, when we lose a job or a relationship ends or we're at the end of our money and the month still has many days left in it or our teenagers are wreaking havoc in our homes that we turn to God. It's when we have nowhere left to turn that we typically turn to Him. I think—*I know*—God would prefer we seek Him all the time, but He will use our dark moments to get our attention if that's what it takes. And if we're smart, we'll take some time out from crying and despair to try to seek God's wisdom for whatever is going on.

These moments of despair and hurt and pain are some of the most important in our entire journey.

Now, let's be clear about one thing: God doesn't *cause* these dark moments or these valleys in our lives. He doesn't take away your job or have your husband kick you out or send an illness just to get us to turn to Him. But sometimes things happen in the world, through the consequences of sin or bad decisions or sometimes due to things completely out of our control—the landlord raises the rent, or a global pandemic stops the world in its tracks—and God uses these circumstances to get our attention and shape us. Romans 8:28 declares that all things work together for our good. That does not mean that all things *are* good, but it does mean that the good, the bad, and the ugly all mix together in this beautiful tapestry called life to eventually come out looking even more beautiful than we could've imagined. There is a plan and purpose for everything going on in your life, whether you see it yet or not.

There is a plan and purpose for everything going on in your life, whether you see it yet or not.

God is our Father. He loves us. He loves us enough to let us mess up. It might feel like he's angry with us or he's punishing us. Scripture does tell us that "the Lord disciplines those he loves, and he punishes each one he accepts as his child" (Hebrews 12:6 NLT). Maybe you've heard your parents say, "This is going to hurt me more than it hurts you," right before you got spanked. Or you may have said it yourself before you had to discipline a child. Well, it actually does hurt to punish our kids, but because we love them so much and want the best for them, we know that we have to do it to teach them valuable lessons.

Have you ever heard the term *helicopter parents*? They're the parents who hover over their kids, afraid to let them fall, making sure every part of their life is easy and smooth. You know what happens to those kids when they get out into the real world, when Mom and Dad aren't there to take care of them? They don't have a clue how to handle things on their own and end up dropping out of college or moving home because they haven't learned at the proper time what it's like to try things and fail and get back up. God is not a helicopter parent. He loves us enough to let us fail, and when we turn to Him, He is there to pick us back up.

The dark periods are also not God's way of punishing you. Instead, our dark moments are simply His allowing us to face the consequences of our actions. Because when we mess up, it can affect our lives and the lives of people we care about, and God doesn't ride in to wave a magic wand and make the pain and messiness all go away. We have to do the work of digging ourselves out of the hole we've created and make whatever changes and restitution that need to happen. But he doesn't leave us alone. If we call to God, He *will* help us through these periods—and God can use them powerfully. Trust me on this one.

WHEN YOU ARE REDUCED TO NOTHING, GOD IS UP TO SOMETHING

When Ron kicked me out, I ended up in a residential counseling facility called Living Waters Ministry in the woods of North Carolina. My friend Denise Boggs, who runs the center, insisted that if I truly wanted healing, I had to fully commit. This involved them taking my car keys away—Ron sent someone to come and drive the car away—and smashing my phone with a hammer. I had no internet, no credit cards. I'd only had time to grab a few things before I left the house, so I was stripped down to the essentials—four pairs of jeans, ten shirts, a few pairs of shoes that didn't even match anything else I brought. I lived in a little bedroom about the same size as my closet at home, and we got to work.

In our daily counseling sessions, Denise started to help me understand my childhood trauma and the ways my early experiences had shaped me. I also learned a lot about the dynamics of our marriage, and why Ron and I couldn't fix the problems in our marriage because we both were so broken from hidden pains of our pasts that we never talked about. I also began to understand, for the first time, that problems in a marriage happen because of both people, and the fact that I never felt I had a voice contributed to my need to find a way to be heard. It all started to unfold right in front of my eyes, and I began to see how I ended up where I did. I also began to see the strategic plan the enemy had been working since I was a child to keep me from becoming everything that God created me to be.

I felt so alone. I knew I had caused incredible pain, but it still hurt that no one seemed to want to check in and see how I was doing. In some ways, the isolation was good—I could work on me and get the help that I needed—but it was devastating in other ways. No one cared about my story, or asked why I'd done what I'd done, or wondered if I was hurting. All arms were wrapped around my brokenhearted husband and family, and I realized that if I was going to get any help, I would have to find it on my own. Just me and Jesus. It was hard. I'm not going to dress it up and make it look pretty, because it was the most painful, gut-wrenching time of my life. I cried so hard for so many days that I wondered if I would ever come out of the grief. I did chores and cleaned the house, cooked meals and fed the horses. I lost twenty-three pounds in thirty days. I call it the devastation diet, and I don't recommend it. And I prayed...I prayed so hard.

And in that little house in the woods, God met me. He didn't leave me to wallow in my own filth. Instead, He allowed me to draw close to Him, and He drew close to me. I had been reduced to nothing, I had been thrown into my own pit and left for dead. Everyone in my life was going on with their lives and I had a choice to make: Would I die here in my brokenness, or would I muster up the little bit of strength and faith that I could find to live? I fasted, and I prayed, and I really opened my heart to the One who knew me while I was still in my mother's womb. The One who chose me before the foundations of the earth were made. I called out to God: "God, if You're really out there, if You are who You say You are, I need You right now like I've never needed You. I need You to help me."

Meanwhile, I was full of doubt. Could I even survive this mess? This devastation? This shame? This failure? The public humiliation? Could God ever use me? Had I gone too far? "Please help me," I prayed. "I want to live and not die. I want to thrive and not just survive. Make me brave and strong and free." That really was my only prayer. I didn't pray that God would give me my marriage back or that I would ever be in ministry again. I just wanted to live the life that God wanted me to live and live it to the fullest.

One day, I was feeling so low I wanted to die, and I went out for a walk on the property. I was desperate at this point. I remember praying that a truck would come down the road and take me out and put an end to my pain. But God didn't send a truck. He sent a flower. As I walked, I saw a flower that had pushed its way up through the asphalt and bloomed right there in the middle of the road. Right in the middle of all the ugly. It was beautiful, and I realized how much pressure it must have taken for that flower to push through the hard stuff that wanted to keep it back. And the Lord said, "If I care about this flower, how much more do I care about you?" He showed me that I would bloom like that, too, one day, even in the middle of all this hard stuff, if I just pressed really hard and trusted Him.

I felt closer to God during that time than I ever had before, and it was powerful. Now, I'm not suggesting you go out and blow up your life as a tactic to get closer to God, but I can tell you that in your deepest, darkest moments, if you call out to God, He will meet you there. Draw close to Him and He will draw close to you. And there is nothing like the peace of being right in the palm of the hand of God, and I would never have gotten there if

> *There is nothing like the peace of being right in the palm of the hand of God.*

everything in my life hadn't fallen apart. I had to become broken before God had the pleasure of molding me into the image He had for me from the beginning.

THE POTTER'S WHEEL

The image of the potter at the wheel shows up several times in the Bible, and I have always loved it. Most of us don't make our own bowls and dishes these days—that's what Target is for (thank you, Jesus)—but this would have been a familiar image in biblical times. A potter would start with a lump of clay on the flat wheel and it would spin around. As the wheel spun, the potter shaped the clay, creating whatever it was he or she wanted to make by shaping and forming it. That's what God does with us. "But now, O Lord, You are our father; we are the clay, and You are our potter; and all we are the work of Your hand" (Isaiah 64:8 NKJV).

In that house in the woods, I gave myself up to God, asking Him to shape me and make me into what He wanted me to become. For so long, I had been trying to tell God what shape to make me, and He had to squash me back down to a lump of clay again so that He could remake me. And when I finally let Him, He didn't reshape me into what I had been before, but into something that looked and felt more like the me I had been searching for all along.

When I drove away from my home and left my family behind, I honestly thought my life was over. But through my potter's wheel experience in that itty-bitty room in the country, I came to realize that falling apart doesn't mean your life is over. When you say, "I quit, God, now it's yours," that's when He can truly start to work. That's when the fun starts.

When you say, "I quit, God, now it's yours," that's when He can truly start to work.

Don't laugh—it's really true. Once you've reached your lowest point and step aside to allow God to work *in you and through you*, this is when God can really get started, and trust me, He likes to do it in amazing and miraculous ways. This is the point in my story where the disaster I had created began to transform into something truly beautiful.

GOD CHOOSES THE UNLIKELY TO DO THE UNIMAGINABLE

Now, you may be wondering, after all that I had done wrong, why would God listen to me? Hadn't I lost my shot at being heard when I rebelled against everything I knew was right?

Not at all. Even then, I understood that the God of compassion does not cease to hear our prayers, even when we screw up. Messing up does not disqualify us from being loved by and heard by God. God is really clear about this: "Therefore, there is now no condemnation for those who are in Christ Jesus, because through Christ Jesus the law of the Spirit who gives life has set you free from the law of sin and death" (Romans 8:1–2). If we are in Christ, He does not condemn us. In fact, if we confess our sin and repent of it, it vanishes—as if it were never even there. "If we confess our sins, he is faithful and just and will forgive us our sins and purify us from all unrighteousness" (1 John 1:9). We are purified and declared clean. The whole concept of the love of God never ceases to amaze me. Why does He love us this way? As much as we try, we can never fully comprehend the depth of love that the Lord has for us. We have never really experienced it from someone on earth, so to try to explain it coming from someone we can't physically touch and feel is so difficult. He just loves us, warts and cellulite and all.

> Messing up does not disqualify us from being loved by and heard by God.

Not only does He overlook our sin and refuse to count it against us, but He also seems to have a special fondness for using the most unlikely people to do His work. Scripture is full of examples of major screwups being chosen to do God's work:

- Noah was a drunk (in Noah's defense, if I'd seen the whole world wiped out and everyone but my family killed, I might be tempted to sneak a margarita as well).
- Abraham was old.
- Jacob was a liar.
- Joseph was abused.
- Moses stuttered.
- Gideon was wimpy.
- Samson loved the ladies.
- Rahab was a prostitute.
- David was a murderer, a schemer, and an adulterer.
- Isaiah preached naked (I can see it now, cover of *Charisma*).
- Jonah ran from God and became fish food before he delivered God's message of repentance.
- Peter denied Christ (multiple times).
- Martha worried about everything (probably would be on Xanax today).
- The disciples fell asleep while praying.
- Zacchaeus was too small (and cheated on his taxes).
- Paul was too religious.

- Timothy was too young.
- Lazarus was dead!

The Bible is chock-full of people who constantly mess up, and God uses them mightily anyway.

One of my favorite stories from the Bible is the prodigal son. Remember this story? It's a parable Jesus told, and it's found in Luke 15:11–32. In it, a father has two sons. One day, the younger one goes to his father and says, "Hey, all this hanging around waiting for you to kick the bucket is really bumming me out. I'd like my inheritance now, please, so I can have fun while I'm young" (my translation). Now, if one of my children said something like that to me, I'd tell them exactly where they could shove their inheritance, but this father agrees, even though his son is basically saying he wishes his father were dead. The younger son thinks, *I'm going to go drink it up and have a grand old time.*

Once he has taken all he can carry, the younger son goes off to a distant country (probably Las Vegas) and squanders all his money on fast cars and women and big houses and parties. But then a famine hits the land where he's living, and the son has no money left and he has to go get a job (ugh!). He gets a job feeding pigs, and get this—he's jealous of the pigs, because at least they're not hungry. Have you ever spent time with pigs? I'm not going to claim to be a farm girl or anything (if you know me, you *know* that's not the case!), but I have been to a farm. Ron's uncles owned pig houses in North Carolina, and we would visit, and let me tell you, *pigs stink*. Also, pigs will eat anything, so most farmers basically give them their leftover scraps. So now the younger son has no food, he's ankle-deep in pig poop, and he's jealous of the garbage the pigs get to eat. After a while, he gets desperate enough to realize the servants in his father's house have enough to eat, and he thinks he'd be better off going home and begging his father to let him be a servant in his home. It would be humiliating, but at least that way, he wouldn't starve to death.

So, he goes home, intending to beg his father to let him be a servant, but as you already know, it doesn't work out quite that way. His father—who this guy said hoped would die—sees his son walking down the road and comes running. He throws his arms around him and kisses him and ugly-cries because he is so glad to see his son again. The son tries to apologize and gets down to start groveling, but the father cuts him off, telling the servants to bring his best robe and put a ring on his son's finger (See? Bling is biblical!) and to kill the fattened calf. He says, "Let's have a feast and celebrate. This son of mine was dead and is alive again; he was lost but now he is found."

The younger son left as a son. He rebelled and left, but when he returned, he returned as a son. Even though he sinned, insulted his father, and basically screwed up his life, it did not make him stop being the father's son. He was in the exact same position when he returned as he was when he left. That's awesome. And that's deliberate. God is telling us here that his sins do not disqualify him from the role he has been assigned. No matter what you've done—no matter how badly you've screwed up—it does not exclude you from the promises God has made or the role God has called you to.

NOW WHAT?

So, God has allowed you to come to a dark place. He uses these moments to get your attention, so that you have nothing left but to trust in Him. Your failures do not disqualify you.

Then what? How do you start to get out of that pit? Well, I can tell you that in my case, it wasn't easy. And it wasn't quick. I didn't just sit around hoping God was going to help me and make me whole. I had to reckon with what I was willing to give up and what I was willing to change to pursue wholeness. I had to swallow hard when my counselor alerted me that this was not going to be an easy fix, nor would it be a quick

> Your failures do not disqualify you.

one. It was going to be painful, and I had to walk through the pain to allow God to heal the pain. We don't want to feel pain, but in my case, God used this painful process to heal me.

The first step in moving toward wholeness is **having the courage to be willing to do whatever it takes**. It is a decision, and you have to be all in. At various points throughout that decade when I was living a double life, I had wanted to stop doing what I was doing. I would promise myself, I'm going to stop acting like this. I'm going to stop doing this. I would pray for help and really intend to change. And for a while, I would stay on the straight and narrow. But then temptation would creep in, and I would make compromises, thinking it wouldn't hurt, just this once. And then, soon enough, I would be back where I started. It was an endless cycle of wanting to be better and then giving in to temptation. It wasn't that I didn't want it enough. The problem was that I wasn't willing to make the kind of sacrifices that would be required to make meaningful change happen.

I have a friend who always tells me she's going to cut back on her drinking. Every few months she will declare herself "on the wagon" and go for a week or two without a glass of wine, which is a huge accomplishment. I'm not diminishing how hard she has to work to get there—I'm proud of her for it, every single time. The problem comes when she is invited to a birthday party, or out for drinks after work, and she finds herself in a situation where she thinks it would be more awkward to not drink, so she ends up ordering a glass, and then, when she gets home, she might have another. The next day, it's easy enough to run by the wine store on the way home and tell herself, "I've had a hard day, it's just this once, I deserve this," and then, you guessed it, the whole cycle starts again.

It's not that she doesn't genuinely want to change her patterns of behavior. It's that she's not willing to cut out the things that are tripping her up. If she wants meaningful change in her life, she might need to say no to the invitations that will put her in the situation where she'll be tempted. She's not there yet. She doesn't want to miss out on important moments in her friends' lives, so she's not willing to stop putting herself in the tempting situations. That's okay. She'll get there, and I'm praying for her and loving her right where she is just like Jesus loved me in my low place.

My point here is not to judge her or anyone—my point is to say that I totally get it. I wasn't willing to make the kind of real sacrifices required to fix my problems until I was no longer given the choice to run away from them. It is hard, and it can be scary to make the decision that you're finally ready to do whatever it takes to make a change. It can be terrifying to say that you're ready to do whatever it takes, no matter the cost, because *it will cost you.*

If you're truly pursuing wholeness, if you really want it more than you want everything that is holding you back, you will have to make sacrifices to get there. In my case, it meant eight months of living apart from my family, with minimal contact. Eight months! And I still had kids in high school, so this meant eight months of not being there to help with homework, with dinners, with seeing them off to the prom. It was eight months of having no phone, no car, no space to call my own. Eight months of having no control over what I ate or what I did with my time and spending hours each day in grueling counseling sessions that opened up deep wounds I would have rather kept closed. It was eight months of not knowing if we would ever be a family again, but knowing that, no matter what happened, something had to change, because the way I had been living was killing me.

Now, in one sense, I didn't really have a choice, because I'd been kicked out. But just because Ron didn't want me living at home didn't mean I had to stay at that counseling center in the hills of North Carolina. I could have left and gone somewhere else where I could have control over my life again, but I didn't. I was so tired of living in pain and the messiness of my sin that I was willing to give up everything to pursue wholeness and freedom. So... here's my second point: To experience real change, you've got to want freedom more than you want the conveniences and routines of your normal life. You may not end up having to live apart from everything you know and love—I pray you don't—but you will still have to be willing to give up *whatever it takes* to find wholeness. If that means smashing your phone with a hammer so you can't text that high school sweetheart you've never quite gotten over, do it. If that means putting a freeze on your credit cards so you can't temporarily buy your way out of pain, do it. If it means putting a tracking app on your phone so your partner can see where you are at all times, do it.

> You've got to want freedom more than you want the conveniences and routines of your normal life.

Another thing you'll have to do is **get rid of your safety net**. In other words, identify the thing or things that you're holding on to that keep you from being totally free. Maybe you're saying, "God, I trust You, take control of my life," but in your heart, you're still holding on to that resentment or unforgiveness because you feel entitled to feel that way because someone hurt you so badly. Maybe you've asked God to take control of your life, but you're still secretly drinking at night before you go to bed because you're so miserable. That is not trust. That is you saying you want to surrender but carving out a portion of your life that you still think is yours.

Nik Wallenda is a seventh-generation tightrope walker, part of the famous Flying Wallendas. You might have seen him on television, walking across Niagara Falls or Times Square or an active volcano on a tightrope. It seems like complete madness to me, but it's also incredible to watch. Because his family has done this for generations, Nik grew up walking on the wire, and he still does it the way his family has always done it—with no safety net. That's right: In his shows, and even when he's walking across the Grand Canyon on a piece of wire one inch thick, there's nothing beneath him to catch him if he falls.

The thing is, sometimes you do fall. Nik's grandfather actually died when he fell off the wire during a stunt. He was walking across a tightrope strung between two ten-story buildings when he lost his balance and fell to his death. And a few years back, the Wallendas were doing a seven-person pyramid (that's a pyramid of seven people, balanced on top of one another, on a tightrope—no thank you!) when one person slipped, and they all came crashing down. No one died, thankfully, but his sister broke every bone in her face and it was a close call for several of them. So, with the very real consequences of missing a step, why doesn't

Nik use a safety net? Because, he says, a net gives you a false sense of security. It's too easy to let your guard down if you know there's something beneath you to catch you if you mess up. When you're walking on that wire without a net, well, every thought will be focused on getting to the other side of that wire safely.

To find true wholeness, you need to get rid of the safety net. In my case, even when I had no phone or ability to make decisions about my day, there was still one thing I was holding on to. At that point, I had one thousand dollars to my name. It was literally all I had, and I was holding on to it for dear life because I didn't know if I was going to have to do life all by myself. It was the money I'd had in my personal bank account, the only one Ron hadn't frozen. I thought it might be all I would have to start my new life if Ron didn't take me back.

To find true wholeness, you need to get rid of the safety net.

Then, one afternoon, I opened my Bible to 2 Samuel 24. In this passage, King David, sitting pretty and proud of how successful his reign has been, orders a census to be taken. It's not totally clear why he does this, but it's likely to show off how big his kingdom has gotten or to show how many men he had who could be conscripted into his army. In any case, what is clear is that God does not like it, and He offers a choice of three punishments for David: seven years of famine, three months of running from Israel's enemies, or three days of plague. God then sends a plague, and seventy thousand people die, and then David gets his act together and begs God to stop punishing his people for his own sin. (Remember? God uses life to get our attention.) God tells David that the way to get the plague to stop is to go buy a threshing floor owned by a guy named Araunah and to build an altar there.

David goes to buy the land, and the owner of the field, Araunah, offers to give it to him for free, and throws in some oxen and yokes for good measure, because, well, David is the king and all, and being nice to the king, especially one who is famous for his armies, is generally a pretty wise move. But David says, "No, but I will surely buy it from you for a price; nor will I offer burnt offerings to the LORD my God with that which costs me nothing" (2 Samuel 24:24 NKJV).

In other words, David knew that if he got the field for free, it wasn't really an offering. It isn't a real sacrifice if it doesn't cost you anything. When I read this story that day, those words jumped off the page and grabbed me by the face. I knew that I had to give an offering to show that I was truly willing to give up the last shred of security I had left and give it all to God. My life had felt so out of control that I was holding on to the one thing I could control, and that money was my lifeline. It was my safety net, and I needed to be able to take a step out onto the wire without the security of that net to catch me if I fell. That afternoon, with hands trembling, I wrote a check for the full amount in my account to Living Waters Ministries. Once I wrote that check and emptied my bank account, I was truly allowing God to be my safety net, and I was showing that I could trust that if I fell, He would be there to catch me.

Now, I know some people will read this story and say that I'm trying to get people to buy their way into God's favor, and let me be clear, I'm not saying that at all. All I'm saying is that I realized that by holding on to that money, I was not giving all of myself up to God. I was trusting in what was in my hand instead of what was in *His* heart for me. When I released the only thing left that made me feel secure, I had to rely completely on His grace.

And that's when the miracles really started.

How about you? Are you ready to really make a change? Are you willing to actually do whatever it takes to find freedom and wholeness? What things are you holding on to that prevent you from fully letting go and trusting God to catch you?

I pray that you will release those things now and see what happens when you really let the potter begin His work.

THINK ABOUT THIS

- God does not cause you to stumble, but He will use your dark moments to mold you if you let Him.
- Messing up does not disqualify you from being used by God. Most of the people in the Bible we regard as heroes of the faith had made mistakes in their past—or their present—but God used them anyway.
- You need to be willing to make the sacrifices to find healing and wholeness. And make no mistake, it will cost you, but it will be so worth it.

SCRIPTURE TO MEDITATE ON

I have been crucified with Christ and I no longer live, but Christ lives in me. The life I now live in the body, I live by faith in the Son of God, who loved me and gave himself for me. (Galatians 2:20)

CHAPTER 6

The Breeding Ground for Miracles

When I finally gave in to God in the little house in the woods and let Him take control of the clay of my life, I started to see changes in how I felt and acted. I started to feel like the broken parts inside of me were beginning to heal, and I started to believe I really might become who God had intended for me to be. I started to believe that I really could do what He wanted me to do and have all that He says I should have.

But I wasn't just praying for and seeking healing and wholeness within me. At this point, I was also praying and begging God for healing for our marriage and our family. I had to believe for my healing first before I could believe for my marriage, but I dared to hope that even after everything I had done, just maybe our marriage and our family could possibly be saved. I really believed that God was changing me, and He could do the same for our marriage.

There was just one problem.

Ron.

I know it's hard to understand, but I loved Ron, I truly did, and I could not imagine a future that did not include him. But Ron did not feel the same way. Ron was hurt, and he was confused, and he was afraid. After the first time I had cheated, he was willing to move on, but after the second time, his trust in me was utterly shattered. I totally understood why. He had not only made up his mind that our marriage could not be saved, but he also told our church that he would not be pursuing reconciliation with me. Ron was *done.*

And I knew Ron. I knew that once he made up his mind, there was no changing it. Ron had always been a man of principles. If Ron told you he was going to do something, he did it. Period. If he told the kids to do something, he expected it to be done or there would be consequences. He was a man of his word, and he had given his word that we were not reconciling, and that was it. And while I was away, there were wild rumors about what had really happened and where I had gone—I was lesbian, a drug addict, in a mental institution in a straitjacket. There was even a rumor that Ron had killed me and buried my body in the woods. I didn't know any of this at the time, but Ron was dealing with all of this madness on top of the hurt and confusion he was feeling about what had really caused me to do the things I had done.

I did everything I could to get Ron to take me back. I begged him. I made promises that things would be different, that I really was changed. I prayed. I fasted. I begged the Lord to change Ron's heart. I would have given anything to have another chance at making it work, but it wasn't up to me. Ron's mind was made up.

I don't blame Ron for this, not one bit. I was the one who had caused the pain, and it was not my place or in my power to tell him he had to let it go. That would be up to Ron. And I knew that Ron would not change his mind on his own. It would take a miracle.

So, obviously I prayed for a miracle.

PEOPLE WILL JUDGE YOU, BUT GOD WILL JUSTIFY YOU

One of the problems with Ron taking me back was that we had a very public ministry. In the years since my private sin was made glaringly public, I've been told over and over—in both overt and subtle ways—that I'm no longer worthy of preaching the gospel or being married to such a great man of God. Some people seem to find pleasure in reminding you of your past and trying to dangle it over your head, but God doesn't. Both Ron and I were suddenly disinvited to many conferences and speaking engagements. Many of our friends distanced themselves from us. And don't even get me started on the social media posts—I can't even look at them. People can truly be horrible online.

It was incredibly painful. It still is. It hurt to have people who we had known and worked with for decades no longer want to hear from us. But I get it—I really do. In Christian ministry, people want their leaders to be people they can look up to. People of character and steadfastness. That's a noble desire, and an understandable one. I, too, want to look up to people of deep faith and strong character. But the reaction we faced is also tied up with the reality of how scared people are to take off their masks and let people see what's really going on beneath. We all fail. We all mess up, in small and big ways, but it is incredibly difficult to be honest about these truths, because there are real consequences for a Christian—church leader or not—when they admit they're not perfect.

The thing that made the situation all the more painful and complicated was that Ron faced the reality that his ministry would be put at risk if he took me back. Through my sin and deception, I was deemed by many to be unfit for the ministry, so if Ron took me back and stood with me, his ministry would be compromised as well. Ron knew that preaching the gospel was what God had created him for and the work God had called him to. He was in a truly impossible situation.

I have known since I was a teenager that I was called to ministry. And the Bible says that my sin—as horrible and damaging as it was—*does not disqualify me* from that calling. I do not have to worry about whether others agree. All I need to do is take God at His word and trust in the promises He has given me. He says I am a new creation (2 Corinthians 5:17). He says my transgressions been blotted out (Isaiah 43:25). He says the iniquity of my sin has been forgiven (Psalm 32:5). He says I am cleansed from all unrighteousness (1 John 1:9). He says, once again, that there is no condemnation for those who are in Christ Jesus (Romans 8:1).

> No matter what you have done or how much pain you have caused or how much you have suffered, it doesn't negate God's calling on your life.

I want you to hold on to these promises too. No matter what you have done or how much pain you have caused or how much you have suffered, it doesn't negate God's calling on your life. It doesn't mean that you don't get to claim God's promises and walk in His truth. And it does not mean that God will not listen to you when you cry out to Him. It doesn't mean that your most precious relationships have to end, no matter what anyone else says. On the contrary, I believe that God's glory and His love shine most brightly in the darkest of places and that He rushes to those prayers and meets our deepest needs in the most miraculous of ways.

GOD WANTS TO HEAL YOUR BADLY BROKEN RELATIONSHIPS

God's perfect mercy allows us to experience healing and restoration to our most damaged relationships, but here are a few things I've learned that I think are helpful when you are living through the pain of a ruptured relationship:

You cannot make the other person change. No matter how much I begged Ron to give me another chance, I could not force him to. No amount of pleading or begging could get him to change his mind. When a relationship is broken, you can only do your part. You can work on yourself, but unless you accept that you are not in charge of another person's feelings, you are only asking for more heartache.

You can apologize and make restitution. But you can't

change another person. We'll go much more deeply into both of these things soon, but for now, please know that they are both necessary for healing in any relationship.

You can pray for the other person. You can ask God to bring healing to them in the same way He is bringing healing to you.

You can pray for the outcome you're longing for. *Lord, I ask that You would give Gayle the courage to trust me again. I ask that You would bring healing to Peter. I ask that You would grant Sarah peace.* This is not time for passive-aggressive prayers: *I ask that You would make Karen realize how wrong she is* or *Please help Frank to see how much he's hurt me.* That's not earnest supplication; that's manipulation. Instead, this is a time to approach God with fear and trembling, knowing that you come to Him as a sinner in need of grace, and pour out your heart.

You are not in control of the timing. It's important to understand this. Here is where most of us get tripped up…God's timing. When we are asking God to do something in our lives, our marriages, our children, our finances, or our health, what we're really saying is *Do it right now! Yesterday!* Remember Sarah and Abraham and Hagar? Sarah just couldn't wait for that promised child because

> You are not in control of the timing.

God's timing didn't line up with hers, and she ended up causing all kinds of heartache. Meanwhile, God was still doing what He said He would. He was just doing it on His own timeline. One thing I've learned about God is this: He is not in a hurry, but He is never late. God's ways truly aren't our ways (Isaiah 55:8–9). I wanted Ron to forgive me, kiss and make up and off we go, but if that had happened, no real change would have taken place in me or in our marriage.

I'm a Southern girl at heart, and I grew up on Southern food. Grits were a staple in my mama's household, and she sure knew how to make them. *Good grits* are made on the stove, boiled for about thirty minutes. You have to add a good bit of salt and butter, and you have to constantly stir the pot (can't have lumpy grits). Well, now they sell instant grits. I tried them…once. Once you've had real grits, you won't tolerate the instant ones. The instant ones are way quicker, but they just do not taste the same. It's the same with instant coffee. I'm a coffee lover, and I know what good coffee tastes like. Opening up a packet of coffee is just blasphemous!

> There are some things in life that just take time, and healing is one of them.

There's an old saying, *Good things come to those who wait*, and I can high-five you on that. There are some things in life that just take time, and healing is one of them, especially if the wound was severe. Imagine going into the hospital for open-heart surgery or brain surgery and being allowed to go home on the same day. We wouldn't even consider that! When a major violation has happened in our lives—a divorce, an affair, an abusive relationship—these things take time to sort through and dig out. It takes time to pour in the antiseptic, stitch up the wound, recover, and heal. You need to know that healing simply takes time so that you don't try to rush God or yourself.

I wish that I could tell you that our healing and restoration came quickly, but it didn't. There were some really good days, but there were also some really, really horrible days when I wondered if we would make it. All I could do while I waited was continue to pray for a miracle.

WHEN THE UNBELIEVABLE BECOMES REALITY

I've been talking about a miracle for a while now, teasing you with the promise of a miraculous story, so how about I get on with it and tell you what happened next?

While I was away at Living Waters Ministry, confronting the

deepest, most frightening depths of my sin and the pain I had caused the people I loved most in the world, it turned out that God wasn't just working on me.

There I was, praying and fasting and begging God to change Ron's mind, desperate for Ron to give me another chance. Ten minutes—literally, just ten minutes—after I wrote that check to my friend Denise for the full amount in my personal bank account, Ron called on the office phone. He said, "Hope, are you all right?"

There was something strange about his voice. It wasn't monotone, like it had been each time I'd heard his voice since he had kicked me out of the house. He was calm and gentle. I told him I was fine, and he told me, "I don't know what this means..."

It was almost like a disclaimer, the way he said it. "What *what* means?" I asked.

But instead of answering that, he said, "And I don't know what it looks like..."

"What *what* looks like?" At this point, my mind was going in a thousand different directions, trying to make sense of what he was saying.

He said, "I've wrestled with God all night, and God told me not to abandon you."

I started to cry right then and there. I mean, it was an ugly cry—big tears and messy globs of snot and everything.

Once again, Ron asked, "Are you all right?"

But I was crying so hard I couldn't even answer, because I was so overcome. I knew, in that moment, that I had gotten the miracle I had been praying for. It was done. We pray for miracles, but when we really show up, they just blow us out of the water.

I don't think the timing of that phone call, not ten minutes after I gave up the last thing that kept me from relying completely and totally on God, was an accident. I truly believe that once I had given up every semblance of control over my life and had honestly and thoroughly asked God to take control and do things His way, He was free to work. When you're at the place where you're willing to give up everything and anything if it leads to healing—that is what I call the breeding ground for miracles.

A few weeks after that first phone call, while I was still living in North Carolina, Ron called again, and he asked if he could take me out on a date. He drove up, and we went to the closest town, up in the mountains of North Carolina. There wasn't much there, just a Walmart and a Red Lobster. He picked me up, we went to Red Lobster, and I promise you I was as nervous as I was on our very first date. After dinner, we walked around Walmart, picking out Christmas presents for our grandbaby, and we held hands. I knew that it was all going to be okay. I didn't know what it would look like or how God would make it happen, but I knew there was hope for us and that God was doing something miraculous and profound in our hearts.

I don't know what you're going through right now. I don't know what road has led you to pick up this book, or what things you're clinging to that keep you from relying completely on God. In my case, it was pain for childhood abuse and rape, the fear of not being perceived as perfect, and a thousand dollars in my wallet. For you, maybe it's a certain relationship or a career path or a hidden sin or words that a family member spoke over you as a child. Whatever it is, I pray you will trust God with it. He is so much greater than you or I can even imagine, and He loves you so much…more than our minds can fathom and our hearts can hold.

> No matter what is in your past, it does not disqualify you—all of you—from the miracles He wants to shower on you.

And I pray that you will know, deep down in your heart, that no matter what is in your past, it does not disqualify you—all of you—from the miracles He wants to shower on you. Your past doesn't make you unworthy or limit what you can do for God. God loves to take screwups just like you and me and use them to do His work. He can use all of you, even the broken parts. And He can heal even the your most deeply broken relationships. You may fear He won't, but He *can* and He *will* make them beautiful if you will give them to Him.

THINK ABOUT THIS

- Work on you; let God work on others. God can't fix what's broken until both people are ready, and you can't make that happen for the other person. All you can do is work on yourself.
- God's desire is for restoration and wholeness. He delights in making all things new. He wants this to work out for you even more than you want it—really.
- God's timeline is usually not the same as ours, and His is so much better. We have to trust that He is going to answer our prayers in His perfect timing.

SCRIPTURE TO MEDITATE ON

He has made everything beautiful in its time. He has also set eternity in the human heart; yet no one can fathom what God has done from beginning to end. (Ecclesiastes 3:11)

CHAPTER 7

Forgiveness from Every Angle

What would you say if I told you that from the moment Ron told me he wouldn't abandon me, everything was awesome? That things went back to normal and our marriage and kids went on happily, bathed in grace and prayer?

Well, if I said all that, I'd be the biggest liar the world has ever seen. Yes, Ron and I were both committed to making our marriage work. True, we both wanted to be faithful to God and each other and to rebuild our family. But it was still really, really hard.

Not long after that Walmart date, Ron brought each of the kids up to see me, and my counselor Denise warned me that I needed to let them say what they wanted to say. I met with each of them individually, and they told me what they wanted me to know about how they were feeling. They were angry, and they were hurt, and they were confused, and I just listened and asked them to forgive me, and then we all hugged, as a family, and it felt so wonderful. And then they left, and I stayed behind, and we all continued to do the hard work of trying to *heal.*

That was the first step—the first of many times they had to forgive me. I had never intended to hurt my children, or even Ron, but when I had acted out of my brokenness, I had hurt them all deeply. But if we truly want to find healing, we can't stay there.

I'm obviously speaking out of my own experience here, and I know that your pain and your mess won't necessarily look the same as mine. But no matter what mistakes you've made or what brokenness you're living with, I can pretty much guarantee that forgiveness will need to be part of your road to healing. Our brokenness and mistakes inevitably cause pain, so where we have hurt, we must ask for forgiveness. Where we have been hurt, we must forgive. Unfortunately, I can tell you from experience that the only path out of your pain comes from embracing the freedom and wholeness that comes from forgiveness.

FORGIVENESS IS NOT AN OPTION

If you want to move toward wholeness, forgiveness is not optional. Asking for forgiveness (genuinely humbling yourself and asking someone to grant pardon for the harm you caused them) and forgiving (making a decision to let go of the hurt and resentment when you have been wronged) is not something you can take or leave.

> If you want to move toward wholeness, forgiveness is not optional.

It's important to note that there is a difference between *offering an apology* and *asking for forgiveness*. An apology is saying you're sorry for what you did to offend someone. Asking for forgiveness is offering an apology and then asking someone to let go of the hurt and pain that your actions caused. It's a lot deeper, and a lot harder to do. But it is essential, and it is the first and most important step toward making things right.

Not forgiving is actually harmful to *you*. There is significant research that shows that holding on to a grudge or an offense can negatively impact your health. Dr. Mason Turner of Kaiser

Permanente says, "Not forgiving someone often leads to hostility towards that person, and your anger and bitterness can seep into other parts of your life. Hostility keeps levels of the stress hormone cortisol elevated in your body, which can trigger a whole range of bad outcomes, including high blood pressure, immune system issues and a tendency to gain weight."[8] On the other hand, letting go of that anger and bitterness can lead to reduced levels of cortisol in your body, which can lead to lower blood pressure, lowered risk of heart attack, lower cholesterol, and better sleep. It can also help reduce anxiety and depression overall. Once again, we see how closely connected your physical and emotional well-being are, and how your health is directly impacted by what's going on in the rest of your life.

But your health is far from the only reason to forgive. Forgiveness is a spiritual imperative. As Christians, we are commanded to forgive. I know that when we have been hurt, we so often want to hang on to that pain and that injustice, because we were the ones who were wronged. But Colossians 3:12–13 (NKJV) says, "Therefore, as the elect of God, holy and beloved, put on tender mercies, kindness, humility, meekness, longsuffering; bearing with one another, and forgiving one another, if anyone has a complaint against another; even as Christ forgave you, *so you also must do*" (emphasis added). As Christians, forgiveness is not optional.

In Matthew 18:21–22, Peter, one of Jesus's disciples, came to him and asked, "How often should I forgive my brother who sins against me? Seven?" I bet Peter was thinking that was pretty generous, offering to forgive someone seven times. I mean, seven times for the same sin? That sounds more than most of us would want to forgive someone. But Jesus answers, "Not seven, but seventy times seven."

Now, I'm no math whiz, but the calculator on my phone tells me that's 490 times. Which is a lot. And I don't believe Jesus was asking the disciples to get out their notepads and mark down each time they forgave until they got to 490, and then they were good. No, I think the point here is that 490 is basically Jesus's way of saying we must forgive infinitely. We are called to forgive as many times as it takes.

Then Jesus goes on to tells a story to illustrate his point. He talks about a king who wanted to settle his accounts with his servants. One servant, who owed him 10,000 denarii (a denarii was about a day's wages), could not pay, so the king ordered that the man, along with his wife and kids, be sold to pay the debt. But the man threw himself down and begged for more time to pay the debt, and the king relented and gave him more time. So then this servant went out and found a man who owed him 100 denarii and began to choke him, demanding payment for what he was owed.

I think most of us understand this impulse—the guy *needed* that cash to save his family. The second man begged him for more time, promising he would come up with the money, but the first servant, even though he was just given more time himself, would not give the same grace to this man and had him thrown into prison until he could pay the debt. Well, the king heard about this and called the first servant back and said, "I forgave you of your debt because you pleaded with me. Should you not also have mercy on your fellow servant in the same way I had mercy on you?" And then he handed him over to the jailers to be tortured until he could repay what he owed. Jesus ends the parable with this: "My heavenly Father will also do the same to you, if each of you does not forgive his brother from your heart" (Matthew 18:35 NASB).

Whoa. It doesn't get more clear than that, does it? If we don't forgive those who have hurt us, God gets upset. But the point here isn't just that we need to forgive—it's *why* we need to forgive: Because we also have been forgiven. When Christ died on that cross for each of us, He forgave us for every single sin that we would ever commit. Because of the blood He shed that day, God has forgiven every one of our sins. With Christ's sacrifice, we have been declared righteous. And if God is willing to forgive us for our sins, how can we not forgive others for theirs?

If we are ever tempted to hold on to a grudge against another, we must remember what God's forgiveness looks like.

- "For I will forgive their wickedness and will remember their sins no more" (Hebrews 8:12).

When we are forgiven, it's as if God *literally can't remember* what we did wrong. It's just...gone.

- "If we confess our sins, he is faithful and just to forgive us our sins and to cleanse us from all unrighteousness" (1 John 1:9 ESV).

When we are forgiven by God, we are cleansed, washed of everything that stains us or makes us dirty.

> If God is willing to forgive us for our sins, how can we not forgive others for theirs?

- "He has not punished us as we deserve for all our sins, for his mercy toward those who fear and honor him is as

> great as the height of the heavens above the earth. He has removed our sins as far away from us as the east is from the west" (Psalm 103:10–12 TLB).

I love this verse. How far are we from our sin once we are forgiven? As far as the east is from the west. That's infinitely far, y'all. East is in one direction, and west is in the other. This is different from north and south—you can travel north only so far (to the geographic north pole) before being forced to travel south; thus, north and south meet at the poles. But east and west never meet; no matter how far you travel east, you will never reach a point at which your next step must be westward. You will never get to the point where you will see the sins you're forgiven of again. That place doesn't exist.

Here's the point: If we are forgiven this much, we have to forgive others who hurt us. Period. It is required of us.

SOME TRUTHS ABOUT FORGIVENESS

Forgiveness may be required of us, but no one said it was going to be easy. Forgiveness may be the hardest thing you're ever asked to do, but that doesn't change the fact that you have to do it. In my case, I wanted Ron and the kids and my church to forgive me—and eventually and graciously, they did—but I also realized that

I needed to be willing to forgive those who had hurt me too. My parents never meant to hurt me, but they did, and in this period, as I came to realize how those early wounds had affected me, I realized that I had to forgive them.

That was hard enough, but then I realized I needed to forgive *everyone* who had hurt me. Really, God?! *All* of them? That boy who raped me when I was fifteen—I have to forgive *him* too?

Yep. That's what these verses mean. I have a genuine *reason* to hold a grudge, but I do not have the *right* to do so. Christ does not give us that right. As I have been forgiven, so I must forgive. *Dang it!* When I look back over the course of my life, it's clear how much the pain and shame of that traumatic event shaped my life, and Jesus wants me to just get over it?

Well, yes and no. For one thing, forgiveness is not about just getting over it. It's about making a conscious choice to let go of the bitterness and pain and hurt, even when those feelings are real and justified. It's about recognizing that even though he did a terrible thing, I, too, have done terrible things that have caused pain for others. It's about recognizing that there was obviously pain in his own life, and trying to understand that he was acting out of his pain in the same way I later did. Remember the phrase *hurt people hurt people*? That boy was Exhibit A. Forgiveness is about recognizing that we are no better or worse than the people who hurt us. I caused immeasurable damage to others, but I believe that I am worthy of forgiveness. If I can believe that about myself, I have to believe it about him as well.

However, forgiveness is not turning a blind eye to damaging behaviors. If you're in a situation where you're being hurt or abused or taken advantage of—well, yes, you will have to forgive the behavior eventually. But you do not have to put up with it. I have a friend whose husband sometimes spends money they don't have on things they don't really need. It's driven out of a need to appear successful, and he always wants to have the right shoes and the best car. The problem is that they don't always have the money to pay the bills, and there are some months when they have to choose whether to pay the electricity or pay the minimum on the credit card. His penchant for retail therapy has damaged her credit as well as his and caused incredible stress in their lives. Now, if he comes to her and earnestly asks for her forgiveness, does she have to forgive him? Yes, ma'am, she sure does. But does she have to

> Forgiveness is not turning a blind eye to damaging behaviors.

give him a pass to continue throwing their money away on things they don't need? Absolutely not.

There is a difference between forgiveness, which is a deliberate decision to let go of feelings or resentment toward someone who has hurt you, and enabling, which is fixing or getting rid of the consequences for someone else's bad behavior, allowing them to continue doing the very thing they have been doing to hurt you. If I had continued to cheat on Ron, he would have needed, from a spiritual perspective, to offer his resentment and hurt feelings to the Lord and let them go in forgiveness, but he would not have been obligated to continue to live with my bad behavior. Do not overlook damaging things that are hurting you or people you love in the name of forgiveness. That's not how this works and it can lead to much more pain down the line. You can forgive others, but you can forgive from another city, state, or country—meaning you can forgive, but you don't have to be in a relationship! If you're married to the person who has caused the offense, you will need 100 percent agreement, from both parties, to move forward and work toward rebuilding trust (we will get to this later on).

And did you see that I said in the last paragraph that forgiveness is a decision? What I mean is, **forgiveness often doesn't start with feelings**. Very rarely does someone feel like they want to forgive another person. Maybe there are some super-holy people out there who manage it, but that's not how it works for me. For most of us, forgiveness is not something we feel first. It's a decision to say, "Yes, you hurt me, but I'm going to let go of the bad feelings and not hold it against you." It starts with your head, with a deliberate choice. The great thing is, once you have genuinely decided in your head to let go, the feelings often follow. Why? Because you have operated in faith and obedience to God, and He rewards you with grace and peace.

Here's another truth about forgiveness: Forgiveness is not a one-and-done kind of thing. Sometimes people make it seem like you forgive someone once, and *poof*, you're healed, and all the bad feelings are gone. Maybe it's like that sometimes. But for us mere mortals over here, it doesn't always work like that. Depending on the seriousness of the fault, you may not have to forgive someone just once. Remember that passage from Matthew—seventy times seven? Ron had to forgive me again and again and again for what I'd done. Months after I had come back home, we'd be watching a movie and adultery would be a part of

> Forgiveness is not a one-and-done kind of thing.

the plot, and he'd have to turn it off because it was too hard to think about. I hurt him deeply, and every time he was reminded of it, he had to make a conscious choice to forgive me all over again. He is a man of deep faith and integrity, and I am so incredibly thankful that he had the spiritual wisdom and grace to make that choice to forgive again and again and again.

HOW TO ASK FOR FORGIVENESS

We all do things we need to be forgiven for, and we are all in a position of needing to forgive regularly. So why are we so bad at asking for it? Have you ever gotten (or given!) an "apology" like this? "I'm sorry you were offended by what I did," or "I'm sorry you took it that way," or "I'm sorry that's how you see it," or "If I hurt you, I'm sorry."

Those are not apologies! That's just saying, *I didn't really do anything wrong, but I'm sorry you didn't like it.* That's not opening up and examining what you have done to hurt someone. It's not an apology if you don't accept responsibility for your part in causing the hurt or offense, even if you didn't mean to. Maybe you didn't think through how your words would sound to the listener, or you didn't intend to make them feel excluded. That doesn't get you off the hook. It doesn't matter if you had no intention of hurting someone—if you did hurt them, you still owe them an apology and you still need to ask for forgiveness. And then *don't do it again!*

Here's what it looks like when you accept your role in causing pain: "I'm sorry for how my words hurt you. I didn't think them through, and I will do better next time. Please forgive me," or "I'm sorry my actions hurt you. That was not my intention, but that doesn't change the fact that you were wounded by what I did. I am sorry and I would be honored if you would forgive me." That's the kind of apology that genuinely shows understanding and remorse.

I hurt *a lot* of people in my sin. You don't sin in a vacuum—it affects everyone around you. It affected my kids, my parents, my friends, our church, and people who didn't even know me. I finally moved back home eight months after Ron and I separated, but our family still had a long way to go, and I had to ask for forgiveness from a lot of people.

First of all, there was Ron. My apology, or apologies, started out with me begging him to please forgive me for all I had done to hurt him. This happened over and over and for many years. I didn't have reasons or explanations for a long time. I just knew I was wrong, and it hurt me deeply to know that I had hurt him so badly. I promised that I would continue to get to the root of all my issues and I would dig as long as it took to make sure this never happened again.

Then there were the children. I wrote them long letters from the counseling center, saying I knew how badly I'd hurt them and asking them to forgive me. Then, as I already mentioned, they came to see me and told me how much I had hurt them, and I listened, even as my heart broke. And then I apologized again and asked them to try to forgive me. Graciously, they all did, though it took some time. That's okay.

I had to ask my parents for forgiveness, and I had to offer forgiveness to them for their actions and how their ways of thinking had unwittingly hurt me. I apologized to Ron's family. Ron's mom is the best human being you'll ever meet, and she told me, "I love you and I don't judge you. You're my daughter and you're always welcome with me." That was so healing. She showed me great love and forgiveness, even after I had trampled all over her son's heart. That was a powerful example of what forgiveness truly looks like.

I also had to ask for forgiveness from my church. This was awful! All of those people looking up at me from the church pews with pain on their faces where they used to look with love and admiration. It broke my heart to let so many people down.

I had to beg forgiveness to many of the church staff members who knew something wasn't right with me for a very long time. Even though they suspected something was up, they had to work for me…in ministry! Some staff left us during this tumultuous time, and that caused me even more pain, but I still begged them to forgive me. Some did. Some didn't. I can understand why they couldn't, and I can't force it. I hope and pray that someday those relationships will experience healing, but for now all I can do is continue to pray and do my best to serve them.

It's also important to forgive yourself. I think this is really the hardest part, because the shame and disgrace and condemnation inside your head can be as overpowering as the knowledge of the pain you have caused others. Forgiving yourself is a daily chore of "bringing into captivity every thought to the obedience of Christ" (2 Corinthians 10:5 KJV). The enemy bombards our minds with "fiery darts" (Ephesians 6:16 NKJV), and we have to take the shield of faith to quench them. We can't let ourselves get sucked into doubting our forgiveness or feeling like we're not worthy. Christ nailed your sins to the cross—all of them—and you have been declared righteous. Try to keep your mind focused on that.

THE HARDEST WORK YOU'LL EVER DO

Forgiveness is not easy. It may be the hardest thing you ever do, depending on how badly you've hurt others or how badly you've been hurt. But it's also the most healing. Offering forgiveness not only frees you from the burden you've been carrying around, but it also opens the way for God to heal you and to restore your relationships. Asking for forgiveness is making yourself vulnerable—you don't know if the other person will accept it or not. But if you're willing to ask, that's the first step toward making things right.

Remember how I told you that when we separated, Ron announced from the pulpit that he would not be pursing reconciliation with me? And do you remember how I asked the church to forgive me? Well, that wasn't the end of the story. Three months after Ron told our church that our marriage was done, he and I walked out onto the stage at Redemption Church holding hands, and Ron announced that we were back together and working to save our marriage. I still tear up thinking about how loud and how long the congregation cheered for us that day. We still had a long road to walk, but forgiveness was what allowed us to take that first step.

Whatever trial you're facing, whatever pain you're holding on to, I truly believe that if you offer it up to God and ask for His help in taking that first step, it will make all the difference in the world.

THINK ABOUT THIS

- Forgiveness is not an option. As Christians, we are commanded to forgive, just as we have been forgiven. End of story.
- Forgiveness is not easy, and it doesn't happen just once. It may take work to truly forgive, and you may need to forgive—or ask for forgiveness—over and over.
- Forgiveness sets you free.

SCRIPTURE TO MEDITATE ON

And when you stand praying, if you hold anything against anyone, forgive them, so that your Father in heaven may forgive you your sins. (Mark 11:25)

CHAPTER 8

Trust: How to Give and Receive Trust

So. You've wrestled with God in the pit, let Him mold you, and worked toward restoring your relationships. Everything will be hunky-dory now, right?

You probably *know* that's not the case. Even if you have truly sought God's path and allowed Him to shape you, even if you've honestly and earnestly forgiven the other person or yourself, it doesn't mean everything in your relationships will magically get better. Once you've asked for forgiveness and it's really been offered, that's not the end of the story. When you've been forgiven—maybe for the first time, maybe for the hundredth time—the next step is rebuilding trust.

Forgiveness, while hugely important, is not the same thing as trust. Forgiveness says, "I let go of the resentment for the pain you've caused me." Trust says, "I am willing to risk opening myself up to let you hurt me again to restore this relationship." Once you've forgiven, then the hard part really begins. You can't get there until you've forgiven or been forgiven, but it's equally important if you want to move past the pain and into healing in the relationship. Rebuilding trust is a slow process, and one that takes deliberate steps.

> Rebuilding trust is a slow process, and one that takes deliberate steps.

Some people are willing to call it a day at forgiveness, because just getting to that place can be such an overwhelming process. If that's where you are, I applaud you. You have done incredible work and I hope you are walking in God's purpose for your life. But if you truly want to embrace the freedom and healing that comes when God makes your mistakes into something beautiful, you need to take the next step and work in rebuilding trust with those you've hurt in your brokenness.

WHAT IS TRUST?

Trust, simply, is knowing and believing that someone's word is good. It's knowing that they're going to do what they say they are going to do. Trust is the confidence that you can lean on, have faith in, and depend on the other person. Trust is believing that the other person will not let you down.

If we have been hurt, violated, or offended, is it truly possible to have this kind of confidence again in the relationship? Absolutely! But not without a great deal of work. Most people aren't willing to do the work, so they cut the person or people out of their lives, ending what could've been a long, meaningful relationship.

Let's be clear—there *are* some people who need to be cut out of our lives, and only you, by the leading of the Holy Spirit, will know what category to place these people in. Why do we want to cut people from our lives after they have broken trust? Let's talk about it.

When you don't have trust in a relationship, you are left with fear. You are afraid the other person is doing the same thing that hurt you before. You fear that you are going to be hurt, that your children are going to be hurt, that things are never going to get better. We've danced around the topic of fear throughout this book, but that's what is really at the heart of everything. We fear we're not good enough, that someone will find out what's really going on, that you won't be strong enough to stand against temptation. Fear is what drives so much of the pain and brokenness in our lives.

I was one big, living, breathing ball of fear for many years. I had lived in such anxiety and fear growing up and it became so ingrained into my brain and emotions that I didn't even know that it was there. I feared authority. I feared friends. I feared I wouldn't be loved, accepted, believed, picked...I feared that if people found out that I wasn't perfect and had issues (just like them) that they would know I wasn't qualified to lead and be in ministry. Fear drove *everything* in my life. The day that I confessed, and it looked like it was over for me...finally I felt the weight of all this turmoil lift from my shoulders because there was nothing else to fear. Everything was out in the open. No more hiding.

But Ron and I were at a crossroads. Could we repair all the damage from the years of lies, hiding, façade? Was it worth putting in the work and the potential for more hurt if Ron put his heart back into my hands?

For us, it was worth it. All of the years, the memories, the hopes and dreams, the kids, the grandkids, our ministry...yes, it was worth it. We loved each other deeply, and we knew that with God nothing is impossible. We took a deep breath, shaking in our shoes, and we said yes to the process of rebuilding trust.

TRUST IS A CHOICE

While forgiveness is not an option, trust is. You have to decide, do I want to rely on this person again, or do I not?

In my case, I knew I wanted to stay married to Ron, and I knew that meant having to rebuild Ron's trust in me. And I knew what a risk Ron was taking by opening himself up to rebuilding a relationship with me. As much as I wanted him to just trust me right away—*I said I was sorry; why can't he believe me when I say I won't do it again?*—it just doesn't work that way. I had to rebuild that trust.

> While forgiveness is not an option, trust is.

Imagine you take a seat in a chair, and it completely falls apart beneath you. You've sat down in this chair a hundred times, and it's always been sturdy, but this time, it just completely falls to pieces beneath you. Someone can take that chair and fix it up and tell you it's as good as new, but are you going to plop yourself right down on that chair? I wouldn't. I would ease my way back into that chair. First, I would press on the arm to see if it held. I would look it over carefully, scrutinizing every joint and every surface. Then I might tentatively put a little weight on it. Eventually, I'd try to let it hold my full weight, but as soon as it creaked a bit beneath me, I'd probably overreact, jumping to my feet, sure it was about to collapse again. It would take me quite a while to trust that this chair would hold my weight again.

It's the same with relationships. Once you've been hurt, it's not easy to trust the other person again. So, what does it look like to rebuild trust in a relationship?

The first step is **scrutiny**. It's examining that chair from every angle, using a flashlight to shed light on every place that has caused harm in the past or might cause harm in the future. I opened myself up to Ron, asking him to examine every aspect of my life, allowing him to poke his nose in wherever he wanted. I held nothing back—I knew I couldn't. If I wanted to rebuild his trust, I had to let him know that there were no secrets, and that I would not hide anything from him.

After scrutiny, the next step is making **restitution**. Restitution, in its most basic terms, is payment for things taken or lost. In our real lives, it doesn't always mean actual payment. I couldn't pay Ron enough to make up for how badly I hurt him, and in any case, we share our money, so that wouldn't have done any good. That didn't mean I didn't owe him, though. I had to find a way to make up for what I'd taken from him. However, in our relationships, true restitution, a signal of a changed heart, does more than just pay back what was owed. In the case of true change of heart, restitution is the process of *giving back more than you've taken.*

Remember Zacchaeus from the Bible? He's the tax collector who wanted to see Jesus in Matthew 19. Now, saying he was a tax collector in those days was basically the same as saying he was a thief. Tax collectors were notorious for taking more than the sum they were sent to collect. It was well known that they lined their pockets with the extra money, so they were hated in those days. The Scripture tells us that Zacchaeus was a tax collector, and it also says he was rich. We don't have to work too hard to figure out where that wealth came from. But he saw Jesus coming along, and he wanted to catch a glimpse of him, but the street was crowded, and "because he was short he could not see over the crowd" (Luke 19:3). (Bit of a Napoleon complex, maybe?)

What did Zacchaeus do? If you spent any time in Sunday school growing up, you know that Zacchaeus climbed a sycamore tree (for the Lord he wanted to see). Jesus saw him up in that tree and said, "Hey, Zacchaeus, come on down, because I'm coming over for lunch!" If someone invites themselves over these days, most of us would consider it rude, but keep in mind, this was Jesus. All those people were lined up to see him, and Jesus singled Zacchaeus out and said, "Hey, buddy, I see you, and I want to get to know you."

So, Jesus came over for lunch, and they had a good time, even though the other people there started gossiping (of course they did) about how Jesus was going to the house of a sinner, as if Jesus didn't already know that, being God and all. We don't know what Jesus said to Zacchaeus during that meal, but we do know that by the end of it, Zacchaeus had offered to sell half of everything he had and give it to the poor. He also said, "If I have cheated anybody out of anything, I will pay back four times the amount" (Luke 19:8).

That's what restitution looks like. It's not just paying back what you owe, or what will rightfully cancel the debt. It's about going above and beyond, trying to make up for the harm you caused and doing it sacrificially.

In my case, restitution meant going to crazy lengths to show Ron how serious I was about rebuilding his trust. I didn't just promise I wouldn't make contact with any men; instead, I didn't buy a phone, so there was no way for anyone to contact me without going through Ron. I didn't get a phone again until Ron brought it up, until he said he was ready to extend that level of trust again. When he finally trusted me enough to say, "Okay, go for it," even then I still made sure to always leave my phone faceup so he could see all the messages that were coming in. He knew my passcode, and I gave him permission to look at it whenever he wanted. In those first two years back home, I didn't make plans to meet up with anyone. I didn't go out for lunch with a girlfriend or go anywhere he wasn't invited. I even called him to let him know I was going to the grocery store, just because I didn't want him to have any doubt about where I was or who I was with. Ron didn't ask these things of me, but I was willing to offer them in the interest of making restitution. Restitution is going overboard. It's going above and beyond and doing whatever it takes. Reconciliation is costly.

After you've done your best to make restitution, the next step is **repeated realities**. This means doing the same thing over and over to show that it is for real. Just like you don't forgive once, you don't earn back trust in one easy step. It means teaching the other person what they can and cannot trust, and it means doing it over and over and over again.

In my case, I couldn't just show up home on time once and expect Ron to trust me completely. I had to show up on time again and again and again. It meant teaching Ron that I would do what I said I was going to do, and it could not happen all at once.

It meant showing him repeatedly that I was going to honor the trust that he had placed in me.

As I learned, trust cannot be rushed. It takes as long as it takes. After about two years of not having a phone, not going out, of doing exactly what I said I was going to do, I'll admit I started to get impatient. I felt like I had proven myself worthy of his trust and couldn't understand why he was withholding it from me. I would say, "I've come so far. Have I not proven myself to you?" And he would say, "I think you should give me the same amount of time to rebuild my trust as you had to violate it."

Trust cannot be rushed.

Which, wow. I mean, I lied to him for almost a decade! Was it really going to take that long to earn back his trust? Thankfully, it did not. But if it had, it would have been all right. I was willing. Trust is easy to lose and hard to rebuild.

How about you? Are you willing to show the other person, again and again and again, that they can trust this new reality? Are you willing to work on rebuilding that trust for as long as it takes? Or are you willing to extend that grace until you can say, with your whole heart, that you trust that other person?

I can tell you for sure, it is not easy. But I can also say that it is worth it, because after repeated realities comes **restoration.** This the good part. This is where God's math comes in. Because restoration is about multiplication.

The prophet Joel tells Israel:

> So, I will restore to you the years that the swarming
> locust has eaten,
> The crawling locust,
> The consuming locust,
> And the chewing locust,
> My great army which I sent among you.
> You shall eat in plenty and be satisfied,
> And praise the name of the LORD your God. (Joel 2:25 NKJV)

First of all, that's a lot of locusts! For a bit of context, you should understand that the book of Joel starts off with a lament over a plague of locusts and severe drought that threatens God's people. The prophet Joel sees these things as God's judgment and urges people to repent. Then he promises that if they repent and turn back to God, God will restore them, even more than they had before. God promises to restore the years the locusts have eaten.

And think about Job. Remember that story? In one of the

stranger stories from the Bible, God bets Satan that no matter what he does to Job, Job will still worship him. Here's how that starts:

> One day when Job's sons and daughters were feasting and drinking wine at the oldest brother's house, a messenger came to Job and said, "The oxen were plowing and the donkeys were grazing nearby, and the Sabeans attacked and made off with them. They put the servants to the sword, and I am the only one who has escaped to tell you!"
>
> While he was still speaking, another messenger came and said, "The fire of God fell from the heavens and burned up the sheep and the servants, and I am the only one who has escaped to tell you!"
>
> While he was still speaking, another messenger came and said, "The Chaldeans formed three raiding parties and swept down on your camels and made off with them. They put the servants to the sword, and I am the only one who has escaped to tell you!"
>
> While he was still speaking, yet another messenger came and said, "Your sons and daughters were feasting and drinking wine at the oldest brother's house, when

> suddenly a mighty wind swept in from the desert and struck the four corners of the house. It collapsed on them and they are dead, and I am the only one who has escaped to tell you!" (Job 1:13–19)

If it were me, I'm pretty sure I would have run if I saw any more servants coming toward me. In the space of just a few moments, Job lost his donkeys, his oxen, his camels, his sheep, his servants—so, basically, all of his wealth—and, worst of all, his children. I would have a hard time getting out of bed, to say nothing of praising God anyway. But not Job. His response was to fall down and worship, saying, "Naked I came from my mother's womb, and naked I will depart. The LORD gave and the LORD has taken away; may the name of the LORD be praised" (Job 1:21). For the next forty chapters, Job wrestles with his losses and listens to his "friends," who try to convince him to turn from God, but Job won't. And so, in the end, God rewards Job for his faithfulness, giving him more than he had before, including fourteen thousand sheep, six thousand camels, a thousand yoke of oxen, a thousand donkeys, as well as seven sons and three daughters (who, the text makes sure to point out, were smokin' hot; so now you know). Because of his faithfulness, God restores what Job had; but remember, by God's math, restoration means you get more than you had before.

In our case, Ron and I didn't get back the marriage we had before. Slowly and carefully and deliberately, we built back a marriage that is so much better than what we had before. After everything that we had been through, we now understood each other better, and our marriage was based on truth and honesty. My relationship with my parents changed completely through this process, as we all worked through our shared grief and scars together. We talked openly and honestly about the temperature in our home while I was growing up and how that had scarred me so severely. We wept together. We repented. We changed. We all grew. What used to be based in fear and the need to perform is now based on shared understanding and love. My relationship with my children changed and is better than ever. We don't hold anything back anymore, but we have all learned to speak the truth in love. This is where God started to turn the mess that I had made into something truly beautiful.

The same can be true for you, whatever it is you're going through. You, too, can build back trust, and though the process is slow and painful and can take much longer than you hope, the restoration that results is so worth it.

IT'S ALL YOURS

When I talk to people about the process of building trust, whether it's in the area of infidelity, spending too much money, or following through on big and small commitments, one of the reactions I often hear is anger and frustration and disbelief. "I'm a grown woman," people say. "I shouldn't have to ask for permission. I shouldn't have to ask my husband if it's okay for me to get a phone. I shouldn't need to account for where I am every moment." Or "I have a job and said I would stick to the budget. I shouldn't need to give him the login information to my credit card account."

The fact is, we don't like being told what to do. I sure don't! And part of what it means to be an adult is that you don't have to ask for permission. I get it. But do you want the good outcome? Do you want the restoration? Then you need to be willing to submit to the scrutiny. You need to be open to figuring out what restitution looks like in your case and offering it, or being willing to accept it. Rebuilding trust means surrendering your rights *willingly*. That last part is key—if it's done with a grudge, with a

> Rebuilding trust means surrendering your rights willingly.

chip on your shoulder, it's not rebuilding trust. If the husband who spends too much resents my friend looking over the credit card bills, it's not rebuilding trust. If you promise to stop looking at pornography and then get annoyed when your spouse checks your browser history, that's not rebuilding trust. The only way to get there is to hold up unclenched hands and say, *It's all yours. Look at it, scrutinize it, check in on me—whatever you need to do, for as long as it takes, until you can trust me again.*

This process is not fun, believe me. It means giving up what is rightfully yours for the greater good. But, oh, the good is so much better than you can ever even imagine. If you are brave enough to plow through the uncharted territory of forgiveness and rebuilding trust, God promises to bless you. God is a great accountant. He always balances the books of our lives.

I love *The Message* Bible. I read it just for sheer pleasure when I'm needing an extra shot of God's love. Look at the promises of God for us in Deuteronomy 30:1–11:

> God, your God, will restore everything you lost; he'll have compassion on you; he'll come back and pick up the pieces from all the places where you were scattered. No matter how far away you end up, God, your God, will get you out of there and bring you back to the land your

ancestors once possessed. It will be yours again. He will give you a good life and make you more numerous than your ancestors.

God, your God, will cut away the thick calluses on your heart and your children's hearts, freeing you to love God, your God, with your whole heart and soul and live, really live. God, your God, will put all these curses on your enemies who hated you and were out to get you.

And you will make a new start, listening obediently to God, keeping all his commandments that I'm commanding you today. God, your God, will outdo himself in making things go well for you: you'll have babies, get calves, grow crops, and enjoy an all-around good life. Yes, God will start enjoying you again, making things go well for you just as he enjoyed doing it for your ancestors.

But only if you listen obediently to God, your God, and keep the commandments and regulations written in this Book of Revelation. Nothing halfhearted here; you must return to God, your God, totally, heart and soul, holding nothing back.

This commandment that I'm commanding you today isn't too much for you, it's not out of your reach. (MSG)

You see that? God wants to restore everything that was lost; not only that, but He also wants to make it better. No matter how far away from Him you get, He wants to bring you back. He wants to give you a good life, a better life than the one you left behind. That's what is on the other side of rebuilding trust. Keep reading, and I'll show you how to get there.

FAITH CAN MOVE MOUNTAINS AND DOUBT CAN CREATE THEM

So far in this chapter, we've been talking about what it looks like to rebuild trust in your relationship with another person. But I don't think you can truly know how to trust another person unless you have first tried to understand what it means to trust in God, and that's much harder. How do you trust someone you can't even see? What does it look like to put your trust in something you can't understand?

One of my favorite stories from the Bible is in Matthew 14. Let's take a minute to understand the context here: Jesus has just learned that His cousin John the Baptist has been beheaded. He goes off to a solitary place to pray, but He has been getting a lot of attention because of these miracles He keeps performing, and the crowds follow Him, and suddenly there are thousands of people there. The disciples, knuckleheads that they are, offer to send the people away because they don't have enough food for them, but Jesus says, "Nah, I've got this," and turns a few loaves of bread and some fish into a meal for five thousand people, and also heals all the sick who are there as well. Which, you know, is a pretty big deal.

After performing this incredible miracle, Jesus sends His disciples off in a boat so He can pray again. Then, when He's done talking to His Father, He gets up and walks out across the surface of the water to catch up with them, as you do. The disciples, understandably, are kind of freaked out and decide it's a ghost. But Jesus says, "Hey, dummies, do you remember how I just fed those five thousand people with, like, nothing? How do you not understand that I can do cool stuff like this?" (You may not find that exact translation in your Bible, but that's pretty much the gist.) But the disciples are a bit slow on the uptake, so Peter says, "Lord, if it's you, tell me to walk out on the water." Jesus replies, "Come."

At which point, Peter steps out of the boat and starts walking toward Jesus. On the surface of the water. Which is pretty much impossible, unless you are walking with Jesus. But then Peter, realizing that he's violating the laws of physics, starts to panic, and immediately begins to sink. He cries out, "Lord, help me!" So Jesus reaches out His hand and catches him and says, "Why did you doubt?"

That simple question says so much, I think. I mean, Peter was literally walking across the surface of the Sea of Galilee. If anyone knew the power of God, it was him, in that very moment! But he started to panic—fear—and sank. But for those few moments, when he stopped listening to the voices in his head that said it was impossible, he was part of one of the most amazing miracles the world has ever seen.

I think trusting in God looks a lot like Peter stepping out of that boat, not knowing whether the water would hold him. It's believing that the God who feeds the five thousand and heals the sick will take care of your needs, even when it seems impossible. When we fix our eyes on Jesus across those waves and decide that the water will hold us, that's trust. And when we start to panic and let fear supplant that certainty? That's when we start to sink.

Note that when Peter does begin to doubt and starts to sink, Jesus doesn't shame him or make him feel bad about it. Jesus helps him. He catches him. He tries to understand: *After all you've seen and everything you know, why can't you trust me?* There is no punishment and no recrimination, no condemnation, just an earnest reminder that Jesus has this under control if Peter will only let Him do His thing.

Trusting in God means ignoring the voices that tell you it's impossible and walking toward the one who tells you to come to

Him. It's believing that your life is in His hands, no matter what. It's knowing that He specializes in doing the impossible. It's telling the enemy, "Not today, Satan. Today, I choose to believe that God truly will work things for my good."

God promises that all things work for the good of those who love him, even our mistakes and terrible decisions and the pain we cause one another. If we can trust in His promise that all things work together for our good, we can step out of that boat without fear that we'll sink.

> Trusting in God means ignoring the voices that tell you it's impossible and walking toward the one who tells you to come to Him.

Take a look at your own life. Are there some areas that you have a hard time seeing how God could possibly fix? What would it look like if you were able to uncurl your fist and say, "God, I don't know how You could possibly fix this, but I'm willing to let you try"? What would it look like if you were brave enough to believe that, even though every past experience says it's impossible, you really can step out of that boat and stand on the surface of the water? If you keep your eyes fixed on Jesus, you truly can.

What are you leaning on instead of trusting Him with every aspect of your life?

What are the fears that are holding you back?

Do you believe it's possible to see healing and trust rebuilt in your relationships?

I believe that God wants to use your mistakes for His glory. If He used mine, He can use anyone's! I believe that God wants to bring restitution and restoration into your life. But for God to make your mess beautiful, you have to trust Him enough to let Him work. God doesn't interfere unless we ask Him to; you need to give Him permission to work. You need to let go of the things you're clinging to and look Him straight in the eye and take a step toward Him, trusting that the God who made the wind and the waves will not let you sink.

There's an old hymn by Bill Gaither that we used to sing, and it's still one of my favorites today. It goes like this:

All I had to offer Him was brokenness and strife.
But He made something beautiful of my life.

My friend, I pray that you are brave enough to step out of

that boat. I pray that you keep your eyes on Him and trust Him enough to let Him do the impossible in your life. I pray that you know that even when you mess up, God will catch you and hold you. And I pray that you would know and believe, with every part of you, that if you let Him, God will use your mistakes for His glory.

THINK ABOUT THIS

- Forgiveness is not optional, but trust is. Rebuilding broken trust takes time and sacrifice, but it's worth it.
- Trust takes time. You can't rush it, no matter how much you want to. And you can't dictate when it's been long enough.
- To rebuild trust, you must be willing to be scrutinized. You have to open yourself up for whoever you hurt to examine every aspect of your life.

SCRIPTURE TO MEDITATE ON

Humble yourselves, therefore, under God's mighty hand, that he may lift you up in due time. Cast all your anxiety on him because he cares for you. (1 Peter 5:6–7)

CHAPTER 9

Can You Really Be Free?

What would your life look like if you didn't worry about your past dictating your future? How would you live if you truly believed, deep down, that God has redeemed your mistakes? That no matter what is in your past, your future is bright? Would it alter how you live day to day? Would it change what you imagine is possible? Would you dream bigger? Dare to imagine a different kind of future for you or your family? Would you take more risks? Apply for that job? Take the next step with that relationship?

What we're talking about in this chapter is freedom. Freedom from the mistakes of our past, freedom from our brokenness, freedom from the sin that holds us back from experiencing God's wholeness and healing, freedom from the lies that you've taken to be the truth. No matter what is in your past, I want you to know that freedom is possible, 100 percent. You with the broken heart, you with the addiction, you with the empty wallet, you with the job you hate, you in the marriage you loathe, you with the pain in your body, you with the sin you can't stop giving in to, you up there in the cheap seats—you can be free from the things that tripped you up in the past. Free to live the glorious, gorgeous, larger-than-life life that God imagines for you.

In fact, freedom is *promised* to us. Galatians 5:1 says, "It is for freedom that Christ has set us free. Stand firm, then, and do not let yourselves be burdened again by a yoke of slavery." It is for freedom that Christ has set us free. He wants us to be free from the yoke (remember that, from chapter 3?) of slavery to sin. Being tied to something—drugs, alcohol, pornography, Little Debbie cakes, Mr. Man-of-My-Dreams-Who-Is-Not-My-Husband, the latest Netflix season of junk, whatever it is—is bondage. We are to be slaves to Christ and nothing else! Freedom is why He died for us. You must be fully convinced of this or you will never be able to fight your way toward the abundant life of freedom that God has already prepared for you long before you ever had a chance to mess up. Get that in your spirit right now—"FREEDOM CAN BE MINE!"

Want more proof? Check out 2 Corinthians 3:17: "Now the Lord is the Spirit, and where the Spirit of the Lord is, there is freedom." If Jesus is the Lord of your life and you have devoted your life to pursing healing, there is freedom there. Right now, tomorrow, and always.

Here's another promise: "If the Son sets you free, you will be free indeed" (John 8:36). I love that *indeed* there at the end. It's like a spotlight pointed at the word *free*, just in case you missed it. If you have been crucified with Christ, if you have submitted to Him and asked Him to be the Lord of your life, you are free. That's true whether you know it or not and whether you believe it or not. Now you will have to pursue your freedom daily, just like you would pursue going to the gym to keep your physical body in shape, but it is yours to take.

Freedom is why He died for us.

In other words, you do not have to ask whether you can be free—you already are. That is promised to you, and God doesn't go back on his promises. Your past? *Poof*—like it never happened. Your sin that keeps you entangled? Gone. You are set free by the blood of Christ Jesus. You already have the freedom you are longing for...but you still have to constantly work on *you*!

The thing is, many of us get caught up and frustrated because freedom doesn't look like many people imagine it will. It's not William Wallace, his face painted blue, shouting, "Freedom!!" It's not even the absence of temptation. Just because you are declared free of the slavery of sin doesn't mean that you won't be drawn to the things that want to entrap you. The body's desires don't go away just because you are free, and the patterns of behavior that led you to where you are don't just magically vanish either.

So what do I mean when I say *freedom*?

WHAT IS FREEDOM?

Here's my definition: *Freedom is continuously pursuing wholeness in your life by pressing toward the high call of God, in Christ.*

Freedom—soul freedom—is recognizing the sins and desires that tempt you to live beneath your calling, dealing with them daily, and pressing toward wholeness. It's about letting go of the things that hold you back and embracing the all-encompassing, all-forgiving, freeing love of Christ. It's about making choices daily that lead you away from temptations and toward healing and wholeness.

Freedom from my past is me choosing, day after day, to make a decision to move past the hurts and scars that led me down the wrong path and choosing instead to serve Christ with my whole heart and to honor my husband and my family. Now, I know some people would say that's not freedom at all—that's being chained to the things in my life. To that I say, having almost lost them all, I will gladly hold on to them as tight as I can.

But more than that, freedom does not necessarily mean the absence of chains. Freedom is about being chained to the right things. It's being chained to the blood of Jesus, which gives you freedom to overcome all the desires and temptations that the devil uses to pull you back. Let's spend a little more time here digging into what that looks like.

> Freedom is about being chained to the right things.

WHAT FREEDOM LOOKS LIKE

Freedom, as I have defined it above, is about dealing with and releasing the sin and desires that hold you back from the life you have been called to. But freedom is not simply avoiding the sin or bad behavior. I have a friend who tends to overeat when she's feeling stressed, or when she's anxious, or when she's happy, or… really, any time. She likes to eat. (Hey, I get it! I like it too!) But more than that, for my friend, overeating is a way of coping with emotions that she doesn't have a healthy way to process. There have been periods of time when she has been able to get her eating under control, and that's something to be celebrated. When she is able to change her behavior, with the help of prayer and counseling and accountability, that's an incredible accomplishment.

But that's not freedom—not yet. Freedom is not behavioral modification. True freedom comes when the desire itself has been crucified. It comes when you no longer have the desire to do the thing that brings you or others harm. That's the hard part! When you desperately want to stop smoking cigarettes and then the urge hits you to grab one...you start pacing, biting your tongue, cramming gum in your mouth, gritting your teeth, and shaking. That, my friend, is torment. That is not freedom. Get the point?

I've heard people say that it's not possible to be free of sinful desires. I've even heard it preached in churches that you can't be free of certain kinds of desires; you can only learn to not give in to them. While I think this teaching is important in many ways—we are most definitely called to turn away from sinful desires when we experience them—it's only telling half the story and missing, in my humble opinion, the most glorious half! I believe that when we commit to continually striving to let go of things that hold us back, when we keep our eyes focused on the goodness that God has for us, that we can, through God's grace, break free not only from sinful *behaviors* but also from sinful *thoughts* and *desires*. This is the freedom that God promises us, and once you've had a taste of that kind of freedom, it's hard to settle for anything less!

> True freedom comes when the desire itself has been crucified.

Now, I will be the first to admit that you won't always succeed. I no longer have any desire to pursue a relationship outside of my marriage. That desire is gone because, through much counseling and discovery, I have dealt with the underlying lies that I believed to be truth that caused me to be broken and drove me to make bad decisions. But I've still got issues. I've still got things I need to offer up to God every single day. My point here is that acting like those desires aren't there is not freedom. It's when the desires have been removed that freedom comes. We must continually crucify our desires and pray for God to remove them so that we can be free from them. That's what continually pursuing wholeness looks like. It's work! However...the prize of freedom is so worth the process.

Let me say this again: Freedom is possible, but it's a lot of work. You probably should have expected that by this point in the book. Nothing worth pursuing comes easily, as we've already seen. And this is no different. I'm not a gym rat, but I used to go to the gym, and I do remember how it feels to actually work on a particular muscle and the awful pain you feel the next day. Science tells us that to actually build muscle, you have to break the muscle down and let it recover, and then it comes back stronger than before. That's what pursuing freedom is like. We have to look at the weaknesses of our lives, hate them enough to be willing to deal with them, put pressure on them, and then let them heal and come back stronger. It's hard, and you have to do it again and again to make a noticeable difference. This is why most people don't live in the freedom that God has already provided for us—we don't like the gym!

> Freedom is possible, but it's a lot of work.

And keep in that mind that, as I like to say, **there's not a place called "there."** What I mean is, you won't ever arrive at a place where you're free from all the things that want to pull you off your path and derail you from pursuing your purpose. But that doesn't mean you stop trying. There's no special nirvana that you can get to where you won't have to deal with people and their issues, or with your own issues. But there is a place called *upward.* There's a place where you're a little closer, every day. Pursuing wholeness is about moving closer to that place all the time.

Also, **freedom isn't really about you**. I know that may sound harsh, but here's what I mean: God doesn't grant you freedom so that you can feel good, although that will happen too. Real, true freedom is not meant as a something that's only for you. Freedom means getting rid of the things that hold you back *so that you can serve God and live out your purpose*. True freedom will always drive you to serve God and serve others.

I want you to take a minute and try to imagine what it would look like if you followed God's call without worrying about your past or about the issues that trip you up day to day. If you could honestly deal with your issues and what's happened before and embrace freedom, what kinds of things could you accomplish for His kingdom?

This, my friends, is what freedom looks like. It's saying, "God, I don't know what you have up your sleeve, but I'm in." Freedom is not about

There is a place called upward.

saying, "I get to decide"; it's saying, "God, You get to decide." You're giving up control so that God can take over, and you'll never expect where He will take you.

BREAKTHROUGH COMES WHEN YOU DECIDE TO BREAK FREE

I can't tell you exactly what freedom will look like in your life. But I can tell you that when you ask God to crucify your desires and bring you there, you will find a kind of freedom you never imagined. It doesn't matter if you are fifteen, thirty, forty-five, sixty, or eighty…you are never too old to surrender to the purpose and plan that God has for your life, and He doesn't go back on His promise of restoring all the lost years.

While Ron and I were separated and I was still living at the counseling center in North Carolina, Denise told me that once your true identity is revealed, all of life's experiences—the good, the bad, and the ugly—will start to make sense. Once we finally let go and release all of the hurt and pain of the past, then we can watch God use all things for our ultimate good (Romans 8:28). Jesus is our role model in this thing called life, so let's just look at His ultimate pain, traumatic experience, and betrayal for a minute. What if Jesus had given up on *His purpose* while He was hanging on the cross, under the weight of all mankind's sin? This was the point of His greatest pain. He was forsaken by His Father, spat on, mocked, and beaten. Even while He endured the pain of the process, He quickly forgave, saying, "Father, forgive them, for they know not what they do" (Luke 23:24 NKJV). He pressed on, didn't give in or give up, and fulfilled His destiny. Now, the same power that raised Jesus from the dead lives on inside of you. I've come to encourage you today that you can do this! You are stronger than you think you are!

I encourage you to take some time to imagine what it would look like if you took off the mask, surrendered your life, and followed God's call without trying to figure out if you're good enough or saved enough or pure enough.

> You are never too old to surrender to the purpose and plan that God has for your life.

The enemy just wants to lie to us and convince us that we're not good enough or smart enough or whatever enough to do it. Did you know that Satan was created for worship? He was the worship leader for the heavenly choir, but his desire for power got him fired and banned from Heaven. He's pretty angry about it, and now he wants to ban you from fulfilling your assignment too. Come on. It's time to recognize who we are fighting and rise up and take back everything the enemy is trying to steal from us. So really think about it. What would you do if you could do anything? What are the things that make your heart sing? What are the skills and talents that God has given you to use for His glory? There are clues there. There is freedom in finding your purpose, in discovering the things God has set aside that only you can do.

Once I had the chance to figure out who I truly was and who God had created me to be, I realized that the clues had been there all along. When I was a girl, my family used to take a vacation every summer to the South Carolina coast, and every year while everyone else was swimming and relaxing, I would be talking to everyone at that hotel pool and making friends with all of them. Interacting with people has always been easy for me, and I love it. That was who I was wired to be, and that was a clue as to what I was created to do. In addition, I have always loved the unlovable, and some called it naïve, but I naturally saw the best in every situation. Those were parts of my makeup that would be important in the ministry I felt called to.

God provides clues for us. Think about your personality and the way you look at life, the things that you are drawn to and the things that grieve your heart. Those are clues as to why you were created and what His desire is for you on this earth.

HOW TO PURSUE FREEDOM

The Bible says, "And just as we have borne the image of the earthly man, so shall we bear the image of the heavenly man" (1 Corinthians 15:49). God's plan for every believer is that we ultimately look like Jesus. Christlikeness. Understand that it's not what we do that gets us into Heaven. Jesus already paid that bill. Paid in full. We cannot produce enough good or righteousness to impress God, but **we are to pursue holiness on this earth**. So let's talk about what that looks like in your real life.

If you want to earnestly pursue freedom, you will need to stay away from the triggers that can push you off course and rob you of joy. What are the things that trip you up? Make a conscious decision to try to avoid them, in the pursuit of wholeness. Remember, we have to crucify our sinful desires, daily, and that's where you'll find freedom.

There are also personal spiritual disciplines that will help keep you walking in the right direction. Spiritual disciplines are things that promote spiritual growth, and they are habits that we have to make a part of our lives every day. Disciplines are things that you do, such as reading God's Word, meditating, praying, fasting, worshipping, serving, learning, tithing, and so on. In 1 Timothy 4:7, it says, "Discipline yourself for the purpose of godliness" (NASB).

Disciplining yourself means spending time each day reading God's Word and striving to understand the Scriptures. If we aren't sure what the next step is, dive into the Word and spend some time reading what God has to say about it. There is power in Scripture that most of us have barely even began to tap.

"Discipline yourself for the purpose of godliness."

Spending time in prayer is also critical. If you aren't talking to God, if you aren't in constant communication with him, how can you ever expect to know His character and hear His direction for you? Don't think of prayer as something you do. Prayer is like going on a date with the love of your life where you talk about anything and everything till three in the morning! Because you love them, you just can't get enough of them (heyyy, that sounds like a rap song). Jesus expects us to pray! He's waiting to talk to you. He misses you. Look at what the Bible has to say about prayer:

- "And when you pray" (Matthew 6:5).
- "But when you pray" (Matthew 6:6).
- "Pray then like this" (Matthew 6:9 ESV).
- "And I tell you, ask...; seek...; knock" (Luke 11:9 ESV).
- "And he told them a parable to the effect that they ought always to pray" (Luke 18:1 ESV).
- "Continue steadfastly in prayer" (Colossians 4:2 ESV).
- "Pray without ceasing" (1 Thessalonians 5:17 ESV).

Should I go on? I think you get the picture.

Ron and I travel a lot, and when we're apart, we call each other every night. We do this because we love each other, because we want to hear each other's voices and make sure that the other is okay, touch base. God commands us to pray with this kind of expectation and hope. He wants to talk to us because He loves us and desires to be near to us.

Worship! Aaah, worship. Worship is focusing on and responding to God, being preoccupied with God. Worshipping God in spirit and in truth is worshipping with both our heart and our head, our emotion and our thought. We must worship privately and publicly, in the congregation of other believers.

All of these spiritual disciplines help to keep us on the road called *upward.* Getting closer and closer to God every day and crucifying all that yucky stuff that seeks to trip us up and keep us from being everything that we're called to be.

Scripture also tells us, above all, to guard our hearts and minds (Proverbs 4:23). There is a young lady on staff at our church who really struggles with anxiety and obsessive thoughts.

> Spiritual disciplines help to keep us on the road called upward.

She texted me the other day and asked me to pray because she had had a sleepless night of worry. I said, "Yes, I'll pray, but what made you worry?" She told me that she had been watching the news and reading a lot about sex trafficking of children and she began to create scenarios in her head about her own kids. I stopped her immediately and said, "Jane, if you know you struggle with anxiety, why on earth are you watching all of this bad stuff on the news?" She said, "Well, I want to stay informed." I was like…no. It is fine to stay *informed*, but more importantly, you need to stay *guarded*!

Let me explain it like this: If you're an alcoholic and you're trying to stop drinking, would you still go to the bar every night? No! You can't keep going back to the source of your temptation. It's not going to be easy, my friend. You will have to set up guards over your ears, eyes, heart, and mind to maintain the freedom that you receive.

Recently our grandson Zayden was spending the night at our place, and he asked me if I wanted to watch a TV show with him. He warned me that it was kinda scary, and I immediately felt that "check" in my gut, but we started the show. Ten minutes into it and I knew this wasn't something we should be watching because it glorified evil, but I decided to use this as a teaching moment. After it was over, Zayden asked if I wanted to watch another episode and I said, "No, I don't think so." He wanted to know why and asked, "Are you scared? Gigi, it's only a show."

I told him that as Christians, God wants us to guard our hearts and not let anything evil into our eyes or ears because it gets into our hearts. Soon, our life starts producing the good or evil that we put into our hearts. I told him those kinds of shows will produce bad dreams and fear and anxiety that wouldn't have been there if he didn't watch the show.

I can promise you 100 percent that suffering (otherwise known as work) will be a part of your freedom. You will have to embrace the fact that you will pay a price to be free. Freedom is never free...It will always cost you. You will more than likely have to lay something down, give up something, or delete some phone numbers or television shows, but it is so worth it.

> Freedom is never free... It will always cost you.

Freedom may look nothing like you imagined it, but it is the key to living the life that God purposed and planned for you...a good life...a beautiful life.

THINK ABOUT THIS

- Freedom is absolutely God's will for your life. He wants you to let go of the things that entangle you and pursue wholeness in Him.
- Freedom comes when *you* decide to break free of the things that are holding you captive. No one else can decide that or do that for you.
- To be free, you must guard your heart by guarding what you let inside and stay clear of temptations. Spiritual disciplines will help you stay on the right path.

SCRIPTURE TO MEDITATE ON

So if the Son sets you free, you will be free indeed.
(John 8:36)

CHAPTER 10

Living Out Loud

If you've made it this far in the book, congratulations. You've probably done some hard work and faced some difficult things you might not have wanted to face. I hope you've been inspired to dig deep into your own life and think about how the messages you learned in your early years shaped you and they are now affecting your adult relationships. You've no doubt wrestled with things in your past you would rather not think too much about and examined the lies that have been tucked into your heart so long you believed they were true. Maybe you've grappled with what it means to forgive or to be forgiven, and how to rebuild trust when it's been destroyed. And I hope with all my heart that you believe freedom is possible. It's what God desires for you most. I can promise you this: If you are brave enough to go through the healing process, you can have the abundant life God desires for you.

I can tell you for sure that I would not want to go through all of my mistakes and all of that pain again. Not for anything. There were days when I wasn't sure I was ever going to stop crying or that my face would ever "go back" to the way it looked before all the tears.

But you know what? Now that I'm on the other side of healing, I can truthfully say that I wouldn't go back and change it if I could. Sure, I would love to spare my family the pain I caused them, but I can see now that I had to break out of the roles I'd been assigned and discover who I really was. After I'd been exposed, I got the chance to find my identity, really for the first time in my life, first and foremost as a daughter of the King. Because that's now at the center of how I'm living, I got the chance to discover who Hope Carpenter really is. And you know what? I like her. It turns out, other people do too. I didn't need to hide who I truly was all that time, but I didn't know how *not to*. Now I can't hide who I am and I don't want to.

Today, my husband and I are more in love than ever and are leading a growing church, and for the first time in my life, I feel like I truly understand who God created me to be, long before I ever made that first mistake. He had to break me to get me here, but it was worth every horrible, painful moment to end up walking in my purpose. I am more than what I went through, but I am still grateful for it. Without the crushing pain, I would not be who I am today and, more importantly, who I am supposed to become.

This can be your story as well—the story of finding the amazing, unique, individual person God created you to be. God can take your brokenness and make something beautiful out of it. God can truly redeem anything, and He wants to use you to fulfill the purpose of God in your life.

Because, remember, freedom isn't just for you. Freedom is about using your gifts to build His kingdom. That's why, as long as I have breath, I'll share about what I've been through to serve God. I hope that hearing my story can help other people take off the mask, find freedom from mistakes and pain, and find their identity in Christ. I fully believe that God can use our not-so-perfect lives for His glory. I believe sometimes He even allows us to go through hard times so that His glory can be revealed.

> God can use our not-so-perfect lives for His glory.

Remember Joseph from the

Bible? He also faced some pretty impossible obstacles. Most of them weren't even his fault, which just makes it feel even more unfair. But what God did through him—well, it changed the fate of the Jewish people. If you haven't read his story in a while, I encourage you to go back and read it now. It's in Genesis 37–50.

Check out verse 37:3: "Now Israel loved Joseph more than all his children, because he was the son of his old age: and he made him a coat of many colors" (KJV).

Joseph, it says, was his father's favorite. That can't have felt good to his eleven other brothers, for sure. But you know what they did about it? Let's just say they didn't take it well. They threw him into a deep, dark pit—all because they were jealous of his jacket.

A jacket! Man, the pain we cause people over such trivial things.

Then Joseph was sold to Potiphar, into the Egyptian military. Joseph must have been so hurt and angry with his brothers and confused about why God had allowed this to happen.

How many times have I looked to Heaven, tears streaming down my face, and asked, "Why?" I had brought most of my pain on myself, and because of what I had done, I had lost everything that was precious to me. But Joseph hadn't even brought this pain on himself. Still, he worked hard and proved trustworthy, and he became the chief servant in Potiphar's house, put over all of his affairs.

But of course, he wasn't home free. He was betrayed again… Potiphar's wife plotted and schemed to seduce Joseph, and when he denied her, she accused him of pursuing her. It was another lie, another accusation. Joseph was thrown into prison, unjustly, after he had worked so hard to make something of a pitiful situation that he didn't deserve or ask for. I'm sure he was overcome with despair and anxiety at this point. I know I would have been.

But Joseph refused to allow outside situations and circumstances to define him. No matter how awful the situations he found himself in, he chose to rise above it and keep fighting. Joseph is my hero. I want to be like him when I grow up.

He got thrown in prison again, but that didn't stop him either. There he went, interpreting a dream, using his gifts. He wasn't sitting in a corner sucking his thumb, ticked off, cursing everybody out and talking about people on Facebook. No, he helped people in whatever situation he found himself in.

Now, it would be such a great story if I told you that because of his good attitude, Joseph immediately got out of that prison and tiptoed through the tulips into his wonderful, trouble-free life. But of course he didn't. He sat in that prison, forgotten again, for two years.

Joseph didn't deserve to go through any of this devastation. But fast-forward to the end of the story. Genesis 50:20 tells us *why* he was allowed to go through it. There was a famine in the land, and its effects stretched into Canaan, where Joseph's father, Israel, and brothers lived. They heard that there was food stored in Egypt, and Israel sent some of his sons to Egypt to buy food. Now, mind you, Joseph had pressed on, waited, had been released from prison, and now had a family of his own. He had, in fact, risen to the position of vizier, which was basically a high-ranking advisor, and was second only to the pharaoh in Egypt. This is exactly who Joseph's brothers had to come to, to beg for food. (Isn't that how God tends to work?) Joseph had reached some degree of a happy, fulfilled life, but there was still something missing. There was no resolution, no answered questions about why he had to go through all that hardship. There was just a past full of pain, regret, and bad memories.

When Joseph came face-to-face with his brothers after all these years, he tested them to see if they felt bad for how horribly they had treated him. He saw the pain on their faces and the tears in their eyes. He saw how much they needed the grain that he could give them—or not.

He could've chosen to withhold the very thing they wanted and needed. He had that power. He had the right.

But Joseph had been through many trials, and trials do something for you that nothing else can. He had seen how faithful God had been to him through it all, and he realized that God had put him in this place for this very moment. Joseph realized that God had allowed him to face trials so that he would understand how important it was to allow restoration and redemption to come full circle.

> God had allowed him to face trials so that he would understand how important it was to allow restoration and redemption to come full circle.

When their eyes met again, with tears streaming down their faces, Joseph said to his brothers, "You intended to harm me, but God intended it all for good. He brought me to this position so that I could save the lives of many people" (Genesis 50:20 NLT).

Did you get that? Joseph recognized that what his brothers did out of jealousy was the same exact thing that God intended to use for good. It wasn't one or the other; it was both. Their selfish actions allowed God to prove how powerful He was. But that's not the whole verse. Keep reading. People often quote that first part, but they leave out the second bit. God didn't just allow bad things to happen to Joseph so that God could show how powerful He is; He allowed bad things to happen so that Joseph could be in the exact right position to save the lives of many people through him.

God took this horrible situation and turned it into something beautiful. Joseph suffered through terrible circumstances, but they were what he needed to go through so that he would be exactly where God wanted him when the time came.

God does that for us too. He uses the terrible situations we face to refine us, strengthen us, and get us to where we need to be to allow redemption and restoration to happen through us.

God loves to take our mistakes, our sins, and the awful things we have to face and use them for His glory. But that doesn't mean it's easy or painless and that it just happens. Joseph had to be ready when the time came, and that meant he had to do the work of forgiving and moving past his pain so his heart could be ready when the Lord called him.

I'm not trying to say my problems were the same as Joseph's. He was sold into slavery by his jealous brothers, imprisoned for things he didn't do, and lied about and betrayed. It's not even in the same category as the mess I made. But I do believe that God still uses the terrible circumstances in our lives—whether we've caused them or not—for His glory.

> God still uses the terrible circumstances in our lives—whether we've caused them or not—for His glory.

In fact, Scripture is *full* of examples of God redeeming people's mistakes to help them walk in their purpose. Remember Jonah? Maybe it's been a while since you heard that story, but there's a whole lot more to it than just a big fish. God had a purpose for Jonah, and He told Jonah very clearly what it was. God told Jonah, "Go to the great city of Nineveh and preach against it, because its wickedness has come up before me" (Jonah 1:2). Jonah was a prophet, and back in those days God used prophets to deliver messages—usually warnings about repentance when they had gone astray—to His people. (I don't know about you, but I sure wish God would be as clear with what He wants me to do as He was with Jonah! I would gladly do whatever He asked if only He would just tell me! Why can't He be as clear and direct these days as He was back then?! But I digress.)

Jonah was told to go to Nineveh to tell the people there they had it all wrong. We're not told what they were doing in Nineveh that was so evil, but other places in the Bible (see the book of Nahum—bet you haven't read that one in a while!) indicate that prostitution, greed, witchcraft, and plotting evil against the Lord were all factors. But Jonah didn't want to go to Nineveh and tell them to return to the Lord, so he got on a boat headed for Tarshish—the exact opposite direction—to "flee from the Lord" (Jonah 1:3). I may not be a Bible scholar, but I'm pretty sure that trying to flee from the Lord is not only a bad idea, but it's also pretty pointless. God is everywhere! You can't run away from God's call for your life, and God was not having any of Jonah's idiocy. The ship encountered a huge storm, so the sailors started throwing cargo overboard to lighten the ship, and they all started calling out to their own gods to save them. All except Jonah, a real class act, who was asleep in the bottom of the boat, blissfully unaware. The captain woke him up and told him to pray to whichever god he served. Eventually, the sailors drew lots to see whose fault the storm was (which seems totally reasonable), and when Jonah came up short, the sailors asked which god he served. He told them, "I am a Hebrew and I worship the LORD, the God of heaven, who made the sea and the dry land" (Jonah 1:9). You have to admit, that's a pretty great answer, no matter what the question was!

When the soldiers heard this, they were terrified, because Jonah had already told them he was running from a task given to him by God. They asked Jonah how to please his god, and Jonah told them to throw him overboard and the storm would stop. To their credit, the soldiers didn't want to toss him over the side of the boat, which meant Jonah would certainly die, and instead tried to row back to shore, but when the storm got worse, they cried out to the Lord—these men who all worshipped their own gods, suddenly praying to Yahweh, the One True God!—and asked forgiveness for what they were about to do. And then, at Jonah's insistence, they threw him overboard, and the storm stopped and the sea grew calm. We're told, "At this the men greatly feared the LORD, and they offered a sacrifice to the LORD and made vows to him" (Jonah 1:16). Do you see that? Even while Jonah was desperately running away from God's purpose for him, God still used his messed-up circumstances to bring these sailors to Him. God used Jonah's mistakes for His own glory. And we haven't even gotten to the whale yet!

Scholars disagree on whether it was a whale or a big fish or some kind of crazy sea monster, but whatever it was, know this: God provided it for Jonah. Scripture says, "Now the LORD provided a huge fish to swallow Jonah, and Jonah was in the belly of the fish three days and three nights" (Jonah 1:17). Jonah wasn't just randomly swallowed by the fish; God put it there to keep him alive so Jonah didn't drown in the sea. Pay attention to this, because it's important: *God didn't abandon Jonah even when he disobeyed Him.* To Jonah, it probably felt like things couldn't get any worse—I don't even want to try to imagine what it would have been like to be inside a fish for three days. But God provided that fish, because even when Jonah was running from Him, God still cared for him and gave him what he needed, even though it may have felt like punishment at the time.

God provided for me in my darkest days. He provided a secluded white house in the middle of nowhere for my incubation and protection, so that I could heal in a private, family setting. God cared for me and loved me to life. He provided people like Lee and Denise Boggs; He provided their grandchildren for me to love on; He provided Debbie Leonhardt and a small Baptist church where nobody even knew my name, along with horses and cows, and rocking chairs on the front porch, and rooms with no internet or television. It might have felt like punishment at times, but God used it all. He knew exactly what I needed, and

God cared for me and loved me to life.

He positioned me exactly where I needed to be for my healing to take place.

Do you ever feel like that? When you're living with the consequences of your bad choices and sin, it can be hard to feel like God is there, but He is. He is providing for you in ways you don't understand and can't even fathom. God wants you to walk in your purpose, and even at your lowest points, He provides for you to get there, even when you can't see it.

Eventually, Jonah got there. While he was there in the belly of the fish, Jonah cried out to God and promised to do what God had called him to do, so God commanded the fish to spit him up onto dry land. God told him once again to go to Nineveh and preach repentance.

This time, Jonah listened, and the people of Nineveh paid attention to his message. They repented and stopped their evil ways and turned back to God. Even though he tried to fight it and messed up in a big way, Jonah surrendered to the Lord, and God used Jonah for the purpose He'd set out for him. Jonah's mistakes did not disqualify him from the purpose God set out for him, and when he even got off track, God used the mess he had made for His glory anyway. *That* should make you get up right where you are and do a happy dance!

Have you ever felt like Jonah? Have you ever strayed so far

from the path you wanted to walk that you didn't know how you ended up there? Have you ever, like Sarah, given up on waiting and taken matters into your own hands? God is still there with you. You cannot possibly go so far off the path that God can't use your mistakes for His glory. It's not possible. He wants to redeem them, and He wants to bring you through them and into His freedom.

I don't know the storms that are raging in your life. I don't know what sin and bondage are holding you back, or what habits you are trying to surrender to Him. But I pray that, today, right where you are, you will trust that the God who made the sea and the dry land will bring you through whatever it is you're facing. I pray that you believe in your innermost being that He will provide for you in the midst of it, and will use you for His glory, no matter what.

THE LIFE IN FRONT OF YOU IS MORE IMPORTANT THAN THE LIFE BEHIND YOU

We started this book at the fiftieth birthday party my church threw for me. Well, I didn't tell you that Ron was supposed to be out of town for that party. I was disappointed, but it was still a party, so I was determined to have a good time. I was dancing around with my grandsons and having a good old time wearing a gorgeous red dress anyway. I was having so much fun goofing around with my church family.

But there was a moment when I looked up and saw my handsome husband walking toward me. Half of his face was covered by a black mask, but I would recognize that man anywhere. I know him so well, heart and soul, that the mask didn't hide who he really was from me. He had flown home to surprise me, and when he walked me out onto that dance floor, I knew that he—finally—could say the same about me. I rested my head on his shoulder and we danced, and it just felt so right. With the mask on, I couldn't lay my head on his shoulder very well, so guess what I had to do? I had to take the mask off. There was no longer any need to hide. I had been exposed, I had lost everything, and in the process I had found the person God had called me to be all along.

I know it's scary to think that you can really be honest and be accepted and loved anyway. But if you can muster up enough faith to believe that your broken places are beautiful to God and lay them at the feet of the potter, He will mold you and make something beautiful out of *your* life too.

I can promise you this: No matter what you're going through, no matter what kind of pain or mess you're in, God can redeem it and use it for His glory. You can't be who you're supposed to be and who you used to be at the same time. If you're tired of living failure to failure and if the treadmill of "presenting perfect" has worn you out, then make a choice today to put in the work to be authentically who God created you to be.

> You can't be who you're supposed to be and who you used to be at the same time.

I pray that you will refuse to let people marginalize you to what you've been through. I pray that you will choose to embrace the crushing and the pain so that all you've been through can shape you into who you're supposed to be. I pray that you let God mold you so that He can use you for His glory *and* the salvation of many (Genesis 50:20).

It won't be easy, but if you're willing to dig in and let God guide your steps, your life will be better than you've ever imagined. No one ever said that our lives would be perfect and without pain, but we are promised that God can, and will, make all things beautiful…if we will let Him.

THINK ABOUT THIS

- God can redeem anything and use it for His glory.
- God will meet you in your darkest times if you have the courage to lay your life down.
- Don't allow the enemy to steal another day from you; rise up and take your life back.
- Let God turn your brokenness into something beautiful.

SCRIPTURE TO MEDITATE ON

You intended to harm me, but God intended it for good to accomplish what is now being done, the saving of many lives. (Genesis 50:20)

Afterword

If you had told me in 2013 that I would be here in 2021, writing a testimony about our marriage, I would have laughed at you. Not because I doubt God, in His redeeming power, but because our marriage was in such a broken place that it seemed impossible to repair.

I really don't have words to describe how devastated I was to find out that my wife had been unfaithful to me and about the double life she lived for so long. I loved my wife. But I just didn't think it was possible to go on like we had been living. I know that no one is perfect, but when you are a pastor and in ministry, the people following you expect you to live your life to a certain standard of godliness. I felt like we had failed so many people. It just all seemed like too much work, and honestly it seemed hopeless.

Here's the thing about God...When we can't go another day, His mercies are new every morning. When we don't have enough strength to whisper His name, He sends us a mustard seed and the mountain is removed. I've seen God work all kinds of miracles throughout my thirty-five years of ministry, but what He did in Hope's life and in our marriage continues to blow my mind! God wrestled with me to get me to a place of surrender, and my conclusion was that I had to at least give God a shot to see if our marriage was repairable.

I would be lying if I told you that it was quick or that it was easy to walk this journey the past eight years. There were days that I cried so hard and so loud that my body physically hurt and my voice was hoarse. There were so many nights in succession that I did not sleep that I thought I was going to have a nervous breakdown. All the while, I was trying to lead a worldwide ministry and be some semblance of a father to our children. I didn't know if I could ever trust my wife again. I wondered if I would remain married to her just because it was the right thing to do. But when I spoke with Hope's counselor, Denise Boggs, she told me, "The woman God is going to send back to you, you have never met." To me, that sounded amazing but also extremely scary.

Fast-forward to 2021, I am happier than I've ever been. I am more in love with my wife than I've ever been. I really don't know why we ever doubt the Lord. His promises are true even when we don't believe them. He is faithful even when we are unfaithful.

Restoration does not mean that you get back what you've lost; restoration means you get back more than what you lost.

I am so proud of my wife. I got a front-row seat to watch her life transform. She is literally a new person. She is fierce and strong, yet gentle and compassionate. Every time the devil thinks that he has knocked her out, she comes back up swinging, determined to be everything that God has called her to be!

I really believe that this book was written to be a tool of transformation for anyone who is struggling with their identity and can't get past hurt and pain. Trust me…Please do not look around you at whatever dire situation you might be in, whether it is your marriage, your health, your bank account, your mental state—whatever it is—and think that it's too big for God! If you would just let go and be willing to do whatever it takes, for however long it takes, God can do the same for you as He did for me and my family. Let Him make something beautiful of your life too.

—Ron Carpenter

Acknowledgments

I went back and forth for months whether or not to write this book. I knew that this would invoke so much pain by revisiting our past. We have come through so many trials in dark days, but I knew that if God would give me the strength to write this book that so many people could be healed.

I have to applaud my children: Chase, Chaz, Chanlin. You were just kids when I was struggling the most. I know there were many days that you did not get what you needed from me as your mother, but you loved me anyway. When everything went public, you were devastated, but you never punched back. My prayer for you is that as you have seen me and your daddy fight for our marriage and fight for our healing and we wouldn't take no for an answer, that it has given you the tools that you will need to fight for your own freedom and healing. You are the greatest gift that God has ever given me.

To my parents, Sandy and Judy Hilley, I love you more today than I ever have. I am so grateful that you loved me enough to be hard on me as a young girl but you also loved me enough to repent later in life for any way that you hurt me. You allowed me the honor to speak the truth in love and uncover generational curses that have changed the entire trajectory of our family line. Our relationship truly exemplifies the restoration of God!

Lee and Denise Boggs...Where would I be without your unconditional love, guidance, impartation, patience, and prayers? You provided a safe place for me to crash and burn and then to heal. Living Waters Ministry is truly a slice of heaven!

Redemption Church...There is nobody like you. You watched me grow up, have babies, do stupid things, learn to preach; you were there during our devastation and you were still there... standing and clapping as we rebuilt. You are my family and one of the loves of my life.

Shelly Boyette. My faithful cheerleader. You never stopped believing in me even when I didn't believe in myself. Only Heaven knows the hours of prayer that have gone up out of your mouth with my name on them. I don't tell you enough how much I love you and how grateful I am for your friendship. We believe in miracles.

Notes

1 https://www.cdc.gov/violenceprevention/childabuseandneglect/acestudy/ace-brfss.html
2 https://www.ajpmonline.org/article/S0749-3797(98)00017-8/abstract
3 This material is borrowed with permission from a book called *God's Love Will Heal Your Heart*, by Denise Boggs and Living Waters Ministry. You can learn a lot more about the ten emotional needs in this insightful and powerful guide. The book is available through Living Waters Ministries or as an ebook.
4 http://www.holocaustresearchproject.org/holoprelude/goebbels.html
5 https://blogs.scientificamerican.com/illusion-chasers/i-heard-it-before-so-it-must-be-true/
6 https://www.psychologytoday.com/us/blog/workings-well-being/201703/how-heal-the-traumatized-brain
7 Ibid.
8 https://wa-health.kaiserpermanente.org/forgiveness-health-benefits/

About the Author

Hope Carpenter is the cofounder of Redemption Church, a megachurch that started in Greenville, South Carolina. The church has satellite locations in San Jose, California; Raleigh, North Carolina; and the Dominican Republic. Additionally, the church reaches people around the world through its television ministry (on the Hillsong channel three times a week and on Daystar every Monday, broadcasting to over 450,000 weekly viewers), ministry app, ministry database, YouTube channel, speaking events, and conferences.

Through Hope Carpenter Ministries, Hope travels to minister women all over the world, including the Dominican Republic, Pakistan, and Argentina. Redemption Greenville has weekly attendance in excess of 20,000, and the San Jose campus has approximately 6,000 attendees. Hope and her husband, Ron, live in San Jose, California.